OLD DOGS REMEMBERED

Also by Bud Johns
  The Ombibulous Mr. Mencken
  Bastard in the Ragged Suit
  What Is This Madness?

Old Dogs Remembered

Edited by Bud Johns

SYNERGISTIC PRESS

San Francisco

The permissions listed on pages 7 and 8 constitute an extension of this copyright page.

The Library of Congress has catalogued the hardcover edition of *Old Dogs Remembered* as follows:
Library of Congress Cataloging-in-Publication Data
Old dogs remembered / edited by Bud Johns. — lst Carroll & Graf ed.
        p.   cm.
    ISBN 0-88184-928-6; $ 19.95
    1. Dogs—Literary collections. 2. American literature. 3. English
    literature.   I. Johns, Bud
    PS509.D604   1993
    810.8'036—dc20   93-7982
    Manufactured in the United States of America   CIP
0-912184-12-4 is the ISBN for this Synergistic Press trade paperback
edition.

Synergistic Press
3965 Sacramento Street
San Francisco, California 94118

Acknowledgments

Contents

Introduction

I knew that when the old dog died I would write about us, but somehow, although I had read many of their pieces, I'd never given a thought to how many others had written of old dogs remembered . . . or how many non-writers had similar deep memories.

An editor friend, a new and devoted dog owner, knew I had resigned myself to the necessity of putting Scoop down and said that he wanted the essay when I wrote it. The piece, which appears in these pages, was a form of therapy —as I'd suspected it would be—but it was also a revelation. Nothing I'd ever written prompted a more intense response.

The night the piece appeared we were preparing to take guests to the airport for a midnight redeye flight when the doorbell rang. A neighbor had been walking his dog and, seeing the lights on, decided to tell me, if I was the Bud Johns who had written that story, how much it had meant to him.

A friend called to say I owed his wife a supply of dry handkerchiefs. The chief executive of a large corporation phoned to say he'd cried because he, too, was going to be taking a favorite old companion on its final visit to the veterinarian.

But what surprised me most was the number of strangers who wrote, in care of the magazine. There were words of appreciation for my writing but the focus was the desire to share their understanding about the loss of an old canine friend. Some sent copies of things they'd written, not for publication but for personal release. Others sent copies they'd clipped of other published pieces, always showing the dog-eared effects of handling, reading, and rereading.

Those clippings made me realize how many writers had dealt with the theme of an old dog lost but not forgotten. The search for their pieces led to the collection which follows.

It should surprise no one that James Thurber and Albert Payson Terhune, men who had little in common except that they were writers who always had dogs and often wrote of them, had addressed the subject. E. B. White and Ross Santee were others. In their cases it was not a question of whether they had written something apropos but which piece or pieces to include.

But the surprises! I'd marveled at the plays of Eugene O'Neill and read Brooks Atkinson's theater reviews but never suspected that the playwright had written "Last Will and Testament of Silverdene Emblem O'Neill" to ease his wife Carlotta's sorrow that their Blemie's days had ended (his biographer erroneously said O'Neill wrote it in anticipation of the death but actually he did so nine days later on December 26, 1940, noting "Everything has gone wrong" since Blemie's death) or that the critic missed his Cleo as I missed my Scoop.

Of course John Burroughs and Louis Bromfield would have had dogs and would have written about them when they were gone. Even knowing that wasn't preparation for the feeling in the former's references to his dogs and his sadness over their deaths—most of which were tragic—in the Journal he began in 1854 at the age of seventeen and continued until his death in 1921.

Burroughs wrote a friend when one dog had a relapse after distemper in 1875. "We expect every hour to be his last. It is almost like losing a child. Indeed, half the people do not mourn so much over the death of their children as we do over Reb. He's a homely cur, but you can hardly imagine how much he has been to us. He has been the life and light of the place for a year." The dog was half black-and-tan terrier and half mastiff, so one can imagine he was indeed "a homely cur."

Burroughs's next Journal entry—and others from the naturalist-essayist's published Journals over a span of more than two decades—traces the emotional impact on an individual who has had—and lost—many dogs.

"Reb is dead (1875), and it seems as if a chapter in my life had closed . . . I may live to be an old man, but I shall not live long enough to forget Reb." Within two weeks Burroughs got Rover, later renamed Rosemary Rose, but two years later wrote: "My beloved dog died this morning from poisoning. I do not need to write in my diary to remember it. It is burnt into my heart." In 1898 it was I–Know, killed by a train, and "I am less grieved than when my other dogs have died, because I have had experience and will not be caught that way again—will not allow a dog to take such a deep hold upon my affections. After a time, I suppose, I can lose dogs without emotion. But how I shall miss that faithful creature from my solitary life; and how long will his memory be fresh in my heart."

Burroughs was wrong about the possibility of losing a dog without emotion. Nine years later he was writing of Nip's death as "one of the worst shocks I ever had and [it] quite stunned me. For a moment the whole universe seemed bereft, and my whole outlook upon life changed . . . I did not know I loved the dog so."

Loudon Wainwright would have understood. He said as much in "Another Sort of Love Story."

"Life gets to be a series of dogs, I thought, and I ticked off those I could remember. Ghosts in the house suddenly. Old dogs . . . I won't live with a lot more dogs, and I won't live with another dog like him."

"Sooner or later, every dog master's memory becomes a graveyard peopled by wistful little furry ghosts that creep back unbidden, at times, to a semblance of their older selves," Terhune commented.

Those "ghosts" sometimes appear as ghosts in the literature. Terhune wrote "Sunnybank's Canine Ghost." Beth Brown, in the preface to her *All Dogs Go to Heaven,* credited the ghost of a wire-haired terrier named Hobo with reviving her career as an author. E. B. White is visited by the ghost of his "dash hound" Fred in "Bedfellows." And there are more.

Fred, who died in Maine at fourteen "after a drink of brandy which he enjoyed," played a comic part in the writer's story "Death of a Pig" and was in one of his last "One Man's Meat" columns. Biographer Scott Elledge even speculates that because of White's "knowing and understanding Fred as well as he did, or thought he did" the dog's "death—as well as his behavior in life—may have indirectly played a part in the creation of *Charlotte's Web.*"

In "Bedfellows," remembering Fred helps White ease into his essay on political concerns, just as recalling Medve provides Thurber with an opportunity to comment on a range of subjects, and Caesar, in the portion of "Death of a Dog" included here, sets the stage for Hudson to recall his first religious training and thoughts about eternal life.

Anyone who has ever cared for a dog (not a "dog-lover" for, as Thurber concluded, that is a dog in love with another dog) has observed what Willie Morris calls "the mysterious chemistry that links a human being and a dog." Nobody has ever described its initial manifestation better than Bromfield when he wrote about his fourth morning with Rex.

Most dog stories end with the death of the dog, Richard Kimball observed many years ago in *The Atlantic Monthly.* Even if one accepts that conclusion (I don't accept it, despite the theme of this anthology. One of my favorites, among those that doesn't, is Morris's "The Saga of Willie and Pete" but I couldn't rationalize its inclusion here because it is a writer writing about his contemporary dog) the variety is enormous. These pages include examples from Thurber, Wainwright, White, Molly Ivins, Ruth Pollack Coughlin, Steve Rubenstein and others who wrote, as I did, just after their loss. White, Thurber, Terhune, Santee and W. H. Hudson ("the most important event of my childhood") recalled past dogs years later.

Hudson, born on the Argentine pampas in 1841 to U.S. citizens, moved at twenty-nine to England where he was naturalized at about the turn of the century. In *Far Away and Long Ago,* published in 1918 four years before his death, he wrote of Pechicko ("doggie"): "Our constant companion and playmate in those days (before he was four) was a dog, whose portrait has never faded from remembrance."

When writers remember old dogs they can be sentimental (even maudlin, although I prefer those who don't go beyond what Thurber calls "a sunset touch") but it isn't always sad. I suspect that readers will break out in broad grins—if not outright laughter—while reading Ivins, Thurber, White, Rubenstein, and others.

The old dogs here remembered are sometimes old in years but not always. Rubenstein's Annie was zero years old when, at eleven months three days, her heart stopped beating on an operating table. White's Daisy was just three when "she died sniffing life, and enjoying it."

There are examples of writers who considered themselves the dog's master in the full sense of the human's superiority and others who weren't so sure. Devotion is frequently a topic. I prefer those who think of it as Bromfield did, in writing of a boxer, as "he may be devoted to you but never in a worshipful way." Or White's description of Fred's "devotion of an opportunist."

Poets of the 18th and 19th centuries seemed especially intrigued by the theme of a dog's death, whether it involved legend or history (e.g. Matthew Arnold's "Geist's Grave," Sir Henry Newbolt's "Fidele's Grassy Tomb," or William Robert Spencer's "Beth-Gelert, The Grave of the Greyhound") or their own experience in the selections included here as "Epitaphs . . . And Such."

Agnes Repplier wrote more than a half century ago, "A lordliness of sentiment mars much of the admirable poetry written about dogs. The poet thrones himself before addressing his devoted and credulous ally." That's certainly not the case with more contemporary examples such as John Updike's "Dog's Death," Robert Creeley's "Hey, Spot," Raymond Carver's "Your Dog Dies," or even T. S. Eliot's "Lines to a Yorkshire Terrier."

It's appropriate the last-named exists, even if it is one of his "minor" poems, because after *Old Possum's Book of Practical Cats* inspired the musical *Cats,* Eliot's widow stressed to an interviewer that she and the Nobel Prize winner had been "dog people."

Although there are examples here of old dogs dying a natural death (Hudson's Dandy "and in his sleep he passed away—a perfect case of euthanasia") it appears that writers are more inclined to turn to the topic if the loss is violent or assisted.

The latter brings into play a number of euphemisms: put down, destroy, put to sleep, put him out of his misery, put away, a push out of life.

The means of this include the vet's needle, a pistol shot, chloroform followed by a dose of strychnine . . . hopefully all humane, although one wonders about Terhune, who granted that it was maudlin (writing in "Fair Ellen of Sunnybank") that he fed his old, blind Sunnybank Sigurdson a pound of cut-up steak and then a pound of lump sugar—both of which the collie loved—before shooting him with a pistol.

Most writers remembering old dogs are recalling their own or ones they were close to but Thurber wrote "Death of a Dog," later reprinted as "Collie in the Driveway," about the family whose car ran over a Terhune collie when they came to pay homage to the author and his Sunnybank Farm in Pompton Lakes, New Jersey.

One reason so many came (Terhune once counted more than 1,700 strangers in one season, saying the intrusion "rips at my nerves and temper") was to see the grave of Lad, marked with a granite block inscribed "Lad, Thoroughbred in Body and Soul."

There are other canine grave monuments mentioned here, including the monument of Lord Byron's, but Ben Hur Lampman ("On Where to Bury a Dog") would most approve of John Galsworthy: "No stone stands over where he lies. It is on our hearts that his life is engraved."

The range of actual burial places for the dogs written about here is extensive: my Scoop overlooking the Pacific, White's Fred in the woodland next to a private dump, Hudson's Dandy "near the second apple tree." O'Neill buried Blemie on a hillside west of Tao House in Northern California, the grave framed by two trees and marked with a headstone bearing the inscription "Sleep in peace, faithful friend."

Ross Santee, as a boy accusing a farm hand of poisoning his dog, learned how others can understand the sadness of such a loss. The man conceded that he'd tried to kick the dog which had bitten him twice "but I wouldn't do a lousy thing like that. I lost the first dog I ever owned that way, somebody poisoned him. I'm sorry about your little dog for I know how you feel."

That was Wrinkle, whose story is included here. Recalling another departed companion, Bing, Santee succinctly wrote what Burroughs's Journal entries had concluded: "No dog ever takes the place of the one that is gone, they make a place for themselves."

Some never hesitate to replace a departed dog (Thurber once began a story: "Probably no one man should have as many dogs in his life as I have had . . .") but with others it's not automatic. Elizabeth Bibesco wrote in "Fido and Ponto": "Fido died. I gave up looking at dogs, alive or china, embroidered or painted . . . And then, in spite of everything, because of everything, a Dalmatian once more involved my life—the life that I had so resolutely determined never again to expose to any dog."

Although this book's theme is the recollection of "old" dogs by writers, the research for it produced one volume (found in the Rare Book Room of the New York Public Library) that was not by a professional author (but perhaps the principal grew up to become one). Still, *Memoriam/ "Fay"/Died/January 15th, 1879* was published—even if done so privately—is in at least one library and is on the subject.

This slim volume opens with a photo of a boy in a hat and overcoat, seated, and a dog on a table with the boy's arm around it. The text begins "Fay was a small dog, of the black-and-tan variety, possessed of rare intelligence and many winning traits, between whom and his master Fred, an unusually warm attachment existed. The following letter relates the particulars of his sudden death and burial:

Blossom Hill, Jan. 19th, 1879

Dear Uncle T.:

I have some very bad news to tell you. Wednesday, Papa, Mama, and Fay went to Marlborough, and when they got back to the village Papa let Fay out to run and get warm, and just as they got to the corner by the Presbyterian church Fay dropped down dead. Papa thinks it was apoplexy. I buried him in the greenhouse. I wrapped him in a cloth and then put him in a nice box filled with fresh shavings. Papa says I can have another dog, but I don't believe they can find another as nice as Fay was. Friskey is well and as fat as ever. I am very sorry about Fay, but I fixed him as well as I could. I think I must stop now.

Your aff. nephew,
Fred"

Then followed an extract from a letter received from Fred's papa: "We have been real sad mourners over the death of little Fay. Fred gave you all the particulars. We miss him very much. He was a dear little dog. It seemed as though it would break poor Fred's heart." A poem ends the little book.

I think the writers represented in these pages would approve of Fred's Memoriam being included for they all understood what Sir Walter Scott meant when he wrote:

"The misery of keeping a dog, is his dying so soon; but to be sure, if he lived for fifty years, *and then died, what would become of me?*"

—Bud Johns

James Thurber

AND SO TO MEDVE

Dog may be man's best friend, but Man is often Dog's severest critic, in spite of his historic protestations of affection and admiration. He calls an unattractive girl a dog, he talks acidly of dogs in the manger, he describes a hard way of life as a dog's life, he observes, cloudily, that this misfortune or that shouldn't happen to a dog, as if most slings and arrows should, and he describes anybody he can't stand as a dirty dog. He notoriously takes the names of the female dog and her male offspring in vain, to denounce blackly members of his own race. In all this disdain and contempt there is a curious streak of envy, akin to what the psychiatrists know as sibling jealousy. Man is troubled by what might be called the Dog Wish, a strange and involved compulsion to be as happy and carefree as a dog, and I hope that some worthy psychiatrist will do a monograph on it one of these days. Even the Romans of two thousand years ago displayed the peculiar human ambivalence about the dog. There are evidences, in history and literature, of the Romans' fondness for the dog, and my invaluable Cassell's Latin Dictionary reveals proof of their hostility. Among the meanings of *canis* were these: a malicious, spiteful person; a parasite, a hanger-on. The worst throw in dice was also known to the Romans as a dog. Caesar may have been afraid he would throw a dog that day he crossed the Rubicon.

Tracing aspersions on the dog in literature and in common everyday speech is a task for some stronger authority than I, such as the Oxford English Dictionary, but there are a few calumnies that I might glance at here, in passing. I remember when "Don't be an Airedale all your life" was a common expression in the Middle West, and a man I knew in Zanesville thirty years ago used the expression a dozen times a day. Shakespeare takes many cracks at Dog from "I would rather be a dog and baying the moon than such a Roman" to "Turn, hellhound!" which Macduff hurls at the bloody Macbeth to start their fifth-act duel with broadswords. The Bard, knowing full well that it is men who are solely responsible for wars, nevertheless wrote "Cry havoc, and let loose the dogs of war!" But it is not only in the classics that the much-maligned hound has been attacked. A craven pugilist is known to boxing fans as a hound. And I have always resented the words Whittier put in Stonewall Jackson's mouth: "Who touches a hair on yon gray head dies like a dog!" Here it is implied that any soldier who took a free shot at Barbara Frietchie would be shot, and shooting is rarely the end of a dog. There are a score of birds and animals which could more aptly have been substituted for the dog and I suggest "Who touches a hair on yon gray head dies like a duck!" But, alas, these ancient libels are past erasing, and Dog will simply have to go on enduring them as patiently as he can.

Stanley Walker, in the old debate of ours that fell so far below the Scopes trial in public interest, condemned the gush that has been written about dogs, as if they and not the female of our own species were the principal object of the sentimental output of men. The truth is that both Dog and Woman have received through the ages undeserved abuse and fulsome praise in about equal measure. But when it comes to the highest praise, for woodwinds, strings, and brasses, Man's favorite theme is the male human being. He describes Woman as a ministering angel, but of himself he cries, "How like a god!"

I wrote somewhere a long time ago that I am not a "dog-lover," that to me a dog-lover is a dog in love with another dog, and I went on to say that liking or disliking varied, in my case, with the individual dog as with the individual person. Comparing the two breeds as such takes a critic onto sensitive ground, where the climate is changeable and the air is stuffy. A discussion of the relative merits of the ape and the wolf would interest me more than a debate about men and canines. In such a debate the dog could not take part, and when Man began to talk loosely about his Best Friend, or himself, I would reach for my hat and find my way to a neighborhood bar.

Most writers on dogs insist on viewing the animal in a human light, as they insist on teaching it tricks that amuse only humans, and the things people admire most in a dog are their own virtues, strangely magnified and transfigured. A man, to hear him tell it, thinks that lying for several days and nights on a grave is the highest possible expression of loyalty, faithfulness, and devotion, and the finest demonstration of grief. Albert Payson Terhune labored to lift the collie not only above all other dogs in sensitivity and awareness, but seemed to have considered its standards of judgment often superior to those of the human being. He actually believed that his collies stalked out of the room in a show of moral disapproval when whisky was poured into glasses, and never considered the strong probability that the dogs couldn't stand the fumes of alcohol in their sensitive and aware nostrils, and just walked away. When my mother used to say that Muggs, our mordant Airedale, could read a man like a book, she always implied that the dog was conversant with the fellow's weaknesses of character. After Muggs had read a man like a book he always growled at him or made his fierce biting leap. In other words, Muggs was a moralist and a reformer, out to punish the weakling and the sinner.

Mother-love, as we call it, the strongest instinct in the female of any species, has always been the most flexible implement in the hands of the sentimentalist. The Scotch collies and the border collies that take part every year in the sheep-dog trials in Scotland are hard-working, well-trained, shrewd sheep dogs whose arduous careers have turned them into realists. I have always believed that human fancy adorned one of my favorite Mother-love legends about these collies. The tale tells that a female that had gone out to bark the cattle home was whelped of half a dozen pups, and promptly tucked five of them under a log, picked up the sixth by the scruff of its neck, and came home behind the cows as always, except for the odd, muffled sound of her bark. She then, of course, led her master back to the log. He had sense enough to take a basket, and the pups were brought home in that. My own conviction, after years of meditation about it, is that the collie left all six pups under the log, brought the cows home, and then led her master to where she had hidden the litter. If you have just delivered six pups, you don't have to carry one of them in your mouth to convince a dog-owner, even a male dog-owner, that a series of blessed events has taken place.

A long time ago, I drove a secondhand Ford sedan up to the Scottish field trials one summer's day. The competition brings together the most experienced sheep dogs of the British Isles. It was won that year, for the second straight time, by an old professional yellow-and-white female with only one eye (maybe she had hidden her puppies under somebody else's log and got a poke in the eye for her intrusion). These dogs have been as carefully educated as bloodhounds or police dogs, and the old-timers go out, bring back six sheep from a distant hill, and put them through all sorts of difficult maneuvers. Each dog is aided only by the whistle signals of his master. Speed and accuracy and smartness of performance count in these sheepdog trials. The day I was there, a young male collie, a novice in sheep-herding, made his debut, went completely to pieces when his sheep refused to enter a small pen at his bidding, promptly sat down on his haunches, and howled to high heaven. He was disqualified but was cheered by the gallery as his master led him away. But let us get back to America.

One day I heard an anthropologist say that a dog gets whatever conscience it has from its master. The eminent scientist almost stumbled into a familiar trap when he began beating the bushes of this tricky terrain: the assumption that the whole pattern of a dog's behavior, even its own familiar rituals and duties, have to be inculcated in the beast by the Great God Man. Anybody who has observed the behavior of a canine bitch and her litter, from whelping to weaning, knows that this particular piece of human pretension is nonsense. Dogs may have only a sensory, and not a historical, memory, they may have to depend on instinct instead of precept, and their reasoning may lack the advantages of accumulated knowledge, but a female dog knows more about raising her own pups (I except only Jeannie) than any man or woman could teach her. A bitch's discipline is her own, and it lacks the pride, idealism, and dreams of the human female, but it works beautifully and with an admirable economy of effort.

This brings us to Medve (Hungarian for "bear"), my first black standard French poodle, whose posture of repose and thoughtful eyes gave her the appearance of a reflective intellectual, absorbed by the mysterious clockwork ticking behind the outward show of mundane phenomena. Her expression, in these moments of meditation, seemed to be one of compassion, as against the deep contemplative look of the bloodhound, whose sadness, more apparent than real, appears to have grown out of a long consideration of Man's queer habit of becoming lost, stolen, wounded, or crooked. We read most of these thoughts into dogs, as we invent other human qualities for them, but anybody who has known dogs well, and studied them fairly, over a period of fifty years, realizes, without being able to prove it, that not all of their peculiar abilities are invented by human romantics. Medve was a dog who could entertain herself and do without human companionship for long hours on end. She liked to retrieve the apples she found in season under the russet tree, but she had just as much fun throwing an apple herself and chasing it as letting me in on the game. She would pull her head far around to the left; give the apple a quick, hard toss, downhill always, and then chase it and bring it back. She liked to go out into the woods by herself, but what solitary games she may have played there I never found out.

Medve was a professional show dog, who once went Best of Breed at the Westminster Show, but she hated public appearances and was happiest living in the country, where she raised two litters of eleven pups each, seven females and four males both times. She was a professional mother, too. One of the pups of the second litter was continually complaining, in the days immediately following its weaning, that it was sick and had to have milk. Medve would patiently examine the pup with practiced expertness, and, satisfied that it was pretending, push it rudely away with her muzzle. Once, when it became unusually obstreperous, she sent it tumbling over and over. It staggered to its feet, put on a show of limping worthy of a ham actor, and announced, in a kind of squeal I had never heard before, that it had been mortally wounded. Medve went over and picked it up and gave it the careful examination that a squirrel gives a nut, turning it over and over carefully. Satisfied, at last, that it wasn't even hurt, let alone dying, she gave it another, but gentler, shove, and stalked out of its presence and into the house.

She could tell, from thirty yards away, the quality and meaning of her puppies' whimpers, screams, squeals, and protests. When an outcry of any kind began, she would lift her head and listen intently. I never learned to tell the difference between one puppy cry and another, but she knew them all. Often she would saunter out to where the puppies were kept, taking her time; once in a while she would run to them swiftly, like a mother who has got an urgent telephone call, but mostly she would just sigh, put her head on her paws, and go to sleep. She managed the tedium of motherhood with the special grace and dignity of her breed. Scotch Jeannie, on the other hand, went around wearing a martyred look when she had pups to care for, as if she had invented parturition and wished she could turn it off, like a faucet. She responded to every call from the puppy basket with a frown of desperation, and I don't believe she could tell a yip from a yelp, or a yap from a yowl. She was a setup for the deceitful tactics of her offspring (she didn't even know how to snap an umbilical cord, and usually asked for human help).

Medve, both times, had more puppies than there was room for at table, as one lady writer has put the not uncommon problem, and she didn't know how to take care of this nutritional situation, as smart as she was. I have collected a dozen romantic newspaper clippings on this subject, the most recent this year about a Great Dane bitch who had fourteen pups and not enough dugs to accommodate them. This animal, according to solemn report, developed a command of mathematics and divided the pups into two groups of seven each, so that there were two separate shifts, or servings. If one of the lustier youngsters came back for a second helping, it seems that he was promptly muzzled away. My own experience with dogs has invariably demonstrated the dietary survival of the strongest, and human control is necessary if the weaker pups are not to be undernourished. If Medve couldn't deal with this predicament, then no other dog could. She never rolled on any of her twenty-two pups and crushed them, but this clumsy disaster is common in the case of Great Danes, bloodhounds, and other females of the larger varieties, as it is with tigresses and lionesses in the jungle. There is no sagacious selectivity in it, either, just pure accident. Medve's conscience, in answering or ignoring the commands of her young, was her inherited own, and none of my business, and probably beyond the comprehension of even the most celebrated anthropologists.

In the case of one of her whelpings, the father of the litter kept hanging around, I forget just why, and, in the manner of the male tiger, he began giving the pups boxing lessons when he thought they were old enough to enjoy rough and tumble. If he got too rough and tumbled one of the pups too far, so that it squeaked, Medve would go for him, with low head and low growl, and nip him on the shoulder and drive him away. The male tiger, incidentally, slips off by himself into the jungle when the female is about to produce cubs, and doesn't return from the bars and the night clubs until the cubs are fairly well grown, thus avoiding sleepless nights, and annoyance in general. Mother-love, in beasts and birds, can't always be observed carefully, because of innate animal secrecy, but—to revisit an old Ohio highway for a moment—I once encountered a mother quail leading her young across the road in single file. She diverted my attention from them by pretending to have a broken wing, and flopped around almost at my feet, in an exhibition of bravura acting something like that of the late Lionel Barrymore as Rasputin. When the small birds had disappeared into the deep grass, she flew calmly away and joined them. The domesticated dog, to be sure, is accustomed to human interference with its young, and will usually tolerate it patiently. Jeannie was a snapper, though—she once broke the neck of a Siamese cat that approached her puppy basket— and I am glad that it was Medve's litter and not Jeannie's which my two-year-old daughter discovered one day in the barn, and began playing with. Jeannie was as inept in a barn with her young as she was in a shoe closet, and once when she lost a pup under a floor board she trotted outside and began frantically digging, with one paw, at the base of the stone foundation. I estimated that she would have reached the skeleton of her pup, by that terrier method, in approximately fourteen weeks. (The same thing happened to Tessa, another Scotty of mine, as I have reported somewhere earlier.) The poodle had sense enough to pry up the floor board in such an emergency, or to ask for help from somebody with muscle and fingers.

A strange phenomenon of family feud, which I was never able to figure out, occurred in the bringing up of Medve's first litter. One of the pups, to me as handsome and genial as any of the others, became an outcast, and its ten siblings continually abused it. In the early weeks Medve always took its part and chastised the attackers, but after they were all weaned she gave the problem no further thought, and I had to drag the culprits away from their victim. The human mother, as I have said before and now say again, devotes her entire life to her young and to her young's young, a life of continual concern and anguish, full of local and long-distance telephone calls, letters and telegrams, restless nights and worried days, but Medve, like all of her ilk, refused to be bothered after the first few months. She once allowed six of her pups, long past the weaning stage, to take a portable victrola apart, scatter records all over the place, and chew off, with active and eager teeth, one leg of an upright ping-pong table, causing a landslide of paddles and balls, books, ash trays, and magazines. As long as the grown pups didn't pester Medve, their life was their own, but if she was badgered, she had a unique way of putting the dog in its place, jumping over it gracefully, and giving it a good cuff on the head with one of her hind paws.

Medve's profound dislike of show business caused her to develop a kind of Freudian car-sickness, because riding in a car had so often meant a trip to a dog show, as did the long and irritating process of trimming. She was made to wear a red rubber bib, tied around her neck, and a newspaper was always placed on the floor of the car. She threw up on it like a lady, leaning far down, looking as apologetic as she looked sick. At one of the last dog shows in which she was entered with two or three of her best male pups, she was reluctant to get up on the bench assigned to her and her family, and so I got up on it myself, on all fours, to entice her to follow. She was surprised and amused, but not interested, and this was also true of my wife, who kept walking past the bench, saying, out of the corner of her mouth, "Get off that bench, for the love of heaven!" She finally got me off, and the dogs on. The dogs all thought it had been a wonderful interlude, except Medve, who, I am sure, had had a momentary high hope that I was going to take her place in the show.

Medve lived to be fourteen, and after she died I wrote a piece about her called "Memorial" for the newspaper *PM,* which died not long afterward. Of the three of us, I am now the only one left. The brief eulogy, written so soon after my bereavement, has a sunset touch here and there, but I have decided not to let my older and colder hand and mind blur its somewhat dramatic feeling. I know now, and knew then, that no dog is fond of dying, but I have never had a dog that showed a human, jittery fear of death, either. Death, to a dog, is the final unavoidable compulsion, the last ineluctable scent on a fearsome trail, but they like to face it alone, going out into the woods, among the leaves, if there are any leaves when their time comes, enduring without sentimental human distraction the Last Loneliness, which they are wise enough to know cannot be shared by anyone. If your dog has to go, he has to go, and it is better to let him go alone. Dogs have little sense of time and they are not comforted by tearful good-bys, only by cheerful greetings. Here, then, with a trace of repetition that I trust will be forgiven, is the piece from *PM*.

James Thurber

MEMORIAL

She came all the way from Illinois by train in a big wooden crate many years ago, a frightened black poodle, not yet a year old. She felt terrible in body and worse in mind. These contraptions that men put on wheels, in contravention of that law of nature which holds that the feet must come in contact with the ground in traveling, dismayed her. She was never able to ride a thousand yards in an automobile without getting sick at her stomach, but she was always apologetic about this frailty, never, as she might well have been, reproachful.

She tried patiently at all times to understand Man's way of life: the rolling of his wheels, the raising of his voice, the ringing of his bells; his way of searching out with lights the dark protecting corners of the night; his habit of building his beds inside walls, high above the nurturing earth. She refused, with all courtesy, to accept his silly notion that it is better to bear puppies in a place made of machined wood and clean blue cloth than in the dark and warm dirt beneath the oak flooring of the barn.

The poodle was hand in glove with natural phenomena. She raised two litters of puppies, taking them in her stride, the way she took the lightning and the snow. One of these litters, which arrived ahead of schedule, was discovered under the barn floor by a little girl of two. The child gaily displayed on her right forearm the almost invisible and entirely painless marks of teeth which had gently induced her to put down the live black toys she had found and wanted to play with.

The poodle had no vices that I can think of, unless you could count her incurable appetite for the tender tips of the young asparagus in the garden and for the black raspberries when they ripened on the bushes in the orchard. Sometimes, as punishment for her depredations, she walked into bees' nests or got her long shaggy ears tangled in fence wire. She never snarled about the penalties of existence or whimpered about the trials and grotesqueries of life with Man.

She accepted gracefully the indignities of the clipping machine which, in her maiden days, periodically made a clown of her for the dog shows, in accordance with the stupid and unimaginative notion that this most sensitive and dignified of animals is at heart a buffoon. The poodle, which can look as husky as a Briard when left shaggy, is an outdoor dog and can hold its own in the field with the best of the retrievers, including the Labrador.

The poodle won a great many ribbons in her bench days, but she would have traded all her medals for a dish of asparagus. She knew it was show time when the red rubber bib was tied around her neck. That meant a ride in a car to bedlam.

Like the great Gammeyer of Tarkington's *Gentle Julia,* the poodle I knew seemed sometimes about to bridge the mysterious and conceivably narrow gap that separates instinct from reason. She could take part in your gaiety and your sorrow; she trembled to your uncertainties and lifted her head at your assurances. There were times when she seemed to come close to a pitying comprehension of the whole troubled scene and what lies behind it. If poodles, who walk so easily upon their hind legs, ever do learn the little tricks of speech and reason, I should not be surprised if they made a better job of it than Man, who would seem to be surely but not slowly slipping back to all fours.

The poodle kept her sight, her hearing, and her figure up to her quiet and dignified end. She knew that the Hand was upon her and she accepted it with a grave and unapprehensive resignation. This, her dark intelligent eyes seemed to be trying to tell me, is simply the closing of full circle, this is the flower that grows out of Beginning; this—not to make it too hard for you, friend—is as natural as eating the raspberries and raising the puppies and riding into the rain.

Brooks Atkinson

CLEO FOR SHORT

She was not an accomplished dog. No tricks, no spectacular rescues, no brilliant achievements—nothing to confound incredulous men. But she was a beautiful and loyal German shepherd dog, and she was infectiously happy. In the course of time she came to be a vital part of our family life. Now that she is gone, our home seems partly desolated. The corners in which she used to doze, smudging the baseboards, look gray and empty; the streets and waste lots where she used to frisk in the morning look dull. When we go to the country the fields seem deserted without her. For the places she most enjoyed took on some of the radiance of her personality and reflected her eagerness and good will.

Since dogs are relatively unimportant in the adult world, it is probably foolish to grieve when they go. But most people do grieve, inconsolably, for a time, and feel restless, lonely, and poor. An epoch in our lives was finished when Cleo (short for Cleopatra) died. Our relationship to the world was perceptibly altered. Nothing else can give us her exultant response to the common affairs of the day. Nothing can quite replace the happy good nature that was always greeting us when we came home or that was mischievously waking us up in the morning, hurrying us out of doors after breakfast, or innocently urging us to go to the country where we all wanted to be.

The place she made for herself in our world was of her own doing. I had no active part in it, particularly in the beginning. Although I am guilty of grieving now, I was innocent of hospitality in her first days among us. One Sunday morning in June when we were living on the farm, my brother called on the telephone. "How would you like to have a puppy?" he casually inquired. "Fine," I said with the heartiness of a man who had never had a dog but was willing to experiment. As an afterthought, "What kind?" I asked. "A police pup," he replied. "She's a stray dog. Been here a week. We don't know what to do with her." "Bring her along," I said, since I was already committed. After all, there could be no harm in a puppy.

About two hours later he drove into the dooryard. A huge, wild animal bounded out of the car and jumped up on me before I could recover my breath. A puppy? Good God, she was alarming! Someone put a pan of water down for her. She lashed into it like a tiger. Someone opened a can of beef. She took the whole canful in two gulps, looking a little hungrily at the arm that fed her. To me, she looked savage and as she ran helter-skelter around the farm all afternoon —about seventy pounds of lightning—I was depressed. "I don't know about this animal," I said mournfully. "After all, I'm no lion tamer."

After her harrowing experience of being a lost dog, Cleo had taken in the situation at a glance, and was eager to settle down in a country household. Our first struggle came at bedtime. Like any other civilized man, I scorned dog-ridden homes, and I proposed to tie her on the porch at night until I could build her a dog house. But that was far from being her idea of the way things were to be. Even while I was tying her, half expecting her to bite me or take me by the throat, she cried with more pathos than I liked, and she bellowed like a heartbroken baby when I put out the lights and went upstairs. Well, a man can't be mean indefinitely. After a miserable quarter of an hour I shuffled downstairs in my slippers to release her, as no doubt she knew I would. As soon as she was free she shot into the house, raced upstairs, and leaped on my bed. That settled our relationship permanently, about twelve hours after we had met. In time I was able to persuade her to sleep in the armchair near my bed or in a bed of her own, but no one ever again proposed to exclude her from any of the privileges of the family.

Since we live in New York most of the year, there was, of course, one other preliminary crisis. We had seen it coming and dreaded it, and no doubt she, too, knew something was in the air. We had intended boarding her with friends and neighbors for the winter: they liked her and would have taken good care of her in the broad country where any sensible dog would want to be. But when at length we started to pack the car one morning to go back to the city, Cleo flew into the back seat and stubbornly stayed there—partly in panic, partly in determination. She could not be expelled without more of a tussle than I had the will to provide. By this time I was more than half on her side. "Let's try her for a few days," I said with some misgivings, and our unwieldy caravan started to roll. Cleo liked the ride home. Cleo liked our apartment; she expanded as soon as she set four feet inside. She was so big and active that she appeared to occupy the whole of it. All evening she was delighted, and before we got up the next morning we heard her scampering and rushing around the living room with the clatter of a happy horse. When we finally emerged from the bedroom the sight was fairly dismaying. She had torn the stuffing out of an upholstered footstool and torn the pages out of a novel that had been affectionately inscribed by the author. But she raised no objections to a little explanatory discipline, and during the rest of her life she never destroyed property again. Although apartment living was confining, she clearly preferred to be with us in any circumstances, and, enormous though she was, she settled down to a city existence like a lady.

Make no mistake about it: the association was intimate. Cleo curled up on her own bed or slyly creeping up on mine on cold nights; Cleo under the breakfast table; Cleo under the writing table when I was working, jiggling my elbow when she concluded I had worked long enough; Cleo impatiently batting the Sunday newspaper out of my hands when I had been reading too long at a stretch; Cleo affectionately greeting the maid in the morning, barking at all the tradesmen, teasing my son or brother to take her to walk at inconvenient moments, going wild with excitement when I picked up the bag that we always took to the country—she absorbed, approved, and elaborated on every aspect of family life.

"Like man, like dog," was her motto. Her determination not to be discriminated against amounted to an obsession. She insisted on being in the bedroom when we slept and in the dining room when we ate. If we went swimming, so did she, ruining peaceful enjoyment. If we shut her in the next room when friends dropped in for the evening she threw herself impatiently against the door until, for the sake of quiet, we released her. Fair enough: that was all she wanted. After politely greeting every guest in turn she would then lie quietly in a corner. "You're a pest," I used to say, generally patting her at the same time. "Go and read a good book," my wife would say with vexation. "What this dog needs is discipline," my mother used to say with tolerant disapproval. To be candid about it, the discipline was easy. Excepting for the essentials, there was none. Cleo could be trusted to do nothing treacherous or mean.

If she had had no personal charm, this close physical association would have been more annoying than endearing. But she was beautiful. Her head, which came up to my waist, was long and finely tapered. Her eyes were bright. Her ears were sharply pointed. By holding them proudly erect or letting them droop to one side she indicated whether she was eager or coquettish. In her best days she had a handsome coat and a patrician ruff at the neck. She stood well and held her tail primly. Her vanity was one of the most disarming things about her. Praise her mawkishly and she fairly melted with gratitude. She was an insufferable poseur. When I came home from work late at night and lounged for a few moments before going to bed, she would sit up erect on the couch, throw out her chest grandly, and draw her breath in short gasps to attract attention. When everyone in the room was praising her—although with tongue in cheek—she would alternate the profile with the full face to display all her glory. "The duchess," we used to call her when she was posing regally in the back seat of the open car. But she was no fool. She knew just how much irony we were mixing with the praise and she did not like to be laughed at. If she felt that the laughter was against her, she would crowd herself into a corner some distance away and stare at us with polite disapproval.

Not that my regard for her was based exclusively on her beauty and amusing personality. She had more than that to contribute; she had a positive value in the sphere of human relations. As soon as she came to the city the orbit of my life widened enormously and my acquaintance also broadened. To give Cleo the proper exercise and a little fun, it was necessary to find a place where she could run loose for an hour. That is how we came to frequent the open piers along the Hudson River. Before she joined our household I had often walked there with a kind of detached enjoyment of a pungent neighborhood. No one ever so much as acknowledged my existence on the piers. But with a big, affable dog as companion, I began to acquire prestige. It was astonishing; it was even exciting. Truck drivers liked to discuss her. Some of the longshoremen warmed up. Policemen took her seriously. The crews of the tugboats took a particular fancy to her. In the course of time they came to expect us around noon, and some of them saved bones and pieces of meat for her refreshment. She was all too eager to jump aboard and trot into the galley, and that delighted them. Eventually Cleo must have had fifty friends along the waterfront, and I had five or six. It was through Cleo that I came to meet Charley, who is one of my best friends, and is always ready for a crack of conversation in the warm office where he dispatches tugboats and distributes the gossip of the river.

On Saturdays and Sundays we explored deeper territory down to the Battery and around South Street, where barges tie up for the winter, or across the river to Hoboken, where ocean vessels dock. When Cleo trotted ahead as a sign of friendly intentions, I discovered that even in these distant quarters I, too, was cordially received, and we had great times together. On weekends we were thus in close touch with important affairs. Hardly a ship could dock or sail without our assistance. Sometimes when we were off our regular beat a tugboat we knew would toot us a greeting as she steamed by. "Hello, Cleo," the skipper would bellow pleasantly from the wheelhouse. A man, as well as a dog, could hold up his head on an occasion like that. Thus Cleo opened up a new life for me, and it was vastly enjoyable for both of us.

There is no moral to be drawn from this tale of Cleo. Although the misanthrope says that the more he sees of man the better he likes dogs, the circumstances are unequal. If Cleo never did a mean thing in her life, there was no reason why she should. Her requirements in life were simple and continuously fulfilled. She was as secure as any dog could be. But men live insecure lives; food and shelter are necessities they work for with considerable anxiety. In a complicated existence, which cannot be wholly understood, they have to use not only their instincts but their minds, and make frequent decisions. They have to acquire knowledge by persistent industry. Their family associations are not casual, but based on standards of permanence that result in an elaborate system of responsibilities. It takes varying degrees of heroism to meet all these problems squarely and live a noble life. Living a life honorably in an adult world is not a passive but a creative job.

For Cleo it was much simpler. As far as I could see, there was nothing creative about it. The food was good; it appeared in the kitchen on time. The house was warm, dry, and comfortable. Her winter and summer clothes came without effort. Her associations were agreeable, including three dogs—all male—of whom she was especially fond. It was easy to maintain a sunny disposition in circumstances like that. But it would be unfair to deny Cleo her personal sweetness and patience. Whether her life was simple or not, she did represent a standard of good conduct. Her instincts were fine. She was loyal and forgiving. She loved everyone in the home. Beyond that, she was joyous and beautiful and a constant symbol of happiness. Although she obviously emulated us, sometimes I wonder. Shouldn't I have emulated her?

Loudon Wainwright

ANOTHER SORT OF LOVE STORY

Right in the middle of a long New Year's weekend full of bright weather on lovely snow and a numbing succession of televised quarterbacks, our dog died. Or to put it absolutely straight, after a family agreement rare in its unanimity, we had his life stopped by a veterinarian who agreed it was the right thing to do for such a painfully and fatally ill old animal. His name was John Henry, but I'm not sure why we'd called him that.

I don't think I have ever been more sharply aware of the fine line between here and gone than I was near the end of when I held him close on the vet's table. The kind doctor, her eyes floating in tears because she knew him and us, pumped something bluish into his leg, and with the calm open-eyed patience that characterized so much of his style, he waited that briefest moment until it struck his center and killed him. A couple of polite gasps and it was over.

Slightly undone by my sentiment and for some wild reason remembering not *Lassie* but *Love Story* and the astounding communicative success of Erich Segal, I will risk a version of his opening question: what can you say about an 11½-year-old dog that died? That he was at least as beautiful as Ali MacGraw. And dumber. And a messier eater. That he ran shining and marvelously fast through fields and rolled snorting in snow and floated a burnt-auburn blur over stone walls. That he didn't much mind Mozart and Bach but that violin solos and harmonicas made him howl. That he could destroy six glasses with one sweep of his tail. That, when I would ask him how he ranked me among the people he liked, he would thump his tail against the floor and grin, occasionally punctuating that with a noise that became a smell. But he was half Irish setter and half golden retriever, and his manners were predictably imperfect.

There was a totally nonhuman quality in his loving. Virtually everyone was a suitable target for his affection, and unlike your one-man brute who will slobber over his master's hand and then dismember the neighbor's child, he menaced nothing, including the rabbits he chased and never got and the skunks who always got him.

Not that he was indiscriminating. He was not a tramp, and he did not follow strangers. He was a wide-ranging country dog, but his daily investigations most always brought him home again at night. He liked to sleep on rugs, usually where it was convenient to stumble over him. He liked to ride in cars. Best, he liked to be invited along on walks, and he worked like a roving scout around the walker —in front, behind, alongside, often at a dead run a good distance away—and when he rested in winter during one of these wonderful dashes in all directions, he would break ice in a stream to cool his belly and his tongue.

Although he was forced to live with a succession of cats, I don't think he liked them at all. Yet in most moods but joy he was a model of understatement. The weary and wary tolerance he displayed at the cats' rude spitting or at their hit-and-run assaults from ambush beneath a chair was the closest he came to expressing real distaste.

Obviously our knowledge is limited about his relationship with other dogs. He probably had wet down bark or bush with every dog within a radius of three miles, but he didn't seem to care much for groups, preferring instead to run alone or with just one other at a time. He was alert and forward but not aggressive, and though his hair bristled splendidly and he growled well when challenged, he had a distinct aptitude for avoiding fights and could walk away from one with a casualness that implied it wouldn't be worth his trouble. In his late years he was treated roughly by a much younger and stronger dog down the road, but he accepted this indignity in a way that wasn't cowardly, as if it were somehow in the normal order of things that the puppy he had earlier taught to play was now bouncing him around quite badly. Even when he was very feeble and old, he always trotted out to defend his home station.

I hope he had a full and happy sex life, but I know only of one affair; it was arranged and he fathered a litter from it. His partner in this matter was a bitch from the household of good friends. She, too, was sweet and easy-going and she looked more or less as if she came from a similarly mixed background. We tell a story about this match and I am no longer sure whether it is entirely true. The story goes that, oblivious of approaching delight, he was taken by car to the vet's for one supervised meeting. The vet said afterward that he felt certain everything had gone well, but perhaps for insurance the two should be brought together again the next day. So next day our dog was put in the car and driven to his appointment, which was once more declared a success. The affair was pronounced consummated—and closed. The dog came home. The following morning he was found ready in the car, presumably awaiting another trip and another meeting.

Unlike Segal's doomed creature, this one wasn't perfect. Now and then his taste in food would turn to garbage and he upset many cans in search for the ripest morsels. He dug holes in lawns and he liked to sprawl on young plants. He was a discoverer of mud. When he found something—often invisible and even nonexistent—to bark at, he barked hard and he ignored commands to stop and come the hell home. I am proud of one area of his ignorance. He knew no tricks at all, unless you count a sort of half-baked pawshake he employed as a last effort in his perpetual and undiscouraged search for affection.

In his last days he had great difficulty getting up, he tottered weakly on three legs and he was dreadfully thin. The pain, even muffled with pills, was leaving him stupid with exhaustion, and it became clear past all reluctance that he needed most a push out of life. Briefly I had the conventional and outlandish thought of doing it myself, and so did one of my sons, who likely loved the dog most. Then, with her potion that hit with such shocking and merciful speed, the doctor ended our nonsense.

That night I dreamed that my son kept calling him. The boy had a way of calling that dog. I woke. Life gets to be a series of dogs, I thought, and I ticked off those I could remember. Ghosts in the house suddenly. Old dogs. When I slept and woke again, it was cold half-light and I was almost sure I heard the dog's toenails against the hall floor and his single, discreet bark to go outside. I won't live with a lot more dogs, and I won't live with another dog like him.

John Galsworthy

MEMORIES

We set out to meet him at Waterloo Station on a dull day of February—I, who had owned his impetuous mother, knowing a little what to expect, while to my companion he would be all original. We stood there waiting (for the Salisbury train was late), and wondering with a warm, half-fearful eagerness what sort of new thread Life was going to twine into our skein. I think our chief dread was that he might have light eyes—those yellow Chinese eyes of the common, parti-colored spaniel. And each new minute of the train's tardiness increased our anxious compassion: His first journey; his first separation from his mother; this black two-months' baby! Then the train ran in, and we hastened to look for him. "Have you a dog for us?"

"A dog! Not in this van. Ask the rear-guard."

"Have you a dog for us?"

"That's right. From Salisbury. Here's your wild beast, sir!"

From behind a wooden crate we saw a long black muzzled nose poking round at us, and heard a faint hoarse whimpering.

I remember my first thought:

"Isn't his nose too long?"

But to my companion's heart it went at once, because it was swollen from crying and being pressed against things that he could not see through. We took him out, soft, wobbly, tearful; set him down on his four as yet not quite simultaneous legs, and regarded him. Or, rather, my companion did, having her head on one side, and a quavering smile; and I regarded her, knowing that I should thereby get a truer impression of him.

He wandered a little round our legs, neither wagging his tail nor licking at our hands; then he looked up, and my companion said: "He's an angel!"

I was not so certain. He seemed hammer-headed, with no eyes at all, and little connection between his head, his body, and his legs. His ears were very long, as long as his poor nose; and gleaming down in the blackness of him I could see the same white star that disgraced his mother's chest.

Picking him up, we carried him to a four-wheeled cab, and took his muzzle off. His little dark-brown eyes were resolutely fixed on distance, and by his refusal to even smell the biscuits we had brought to make him happy, we knew that the human being had not yet come into a life that had contained so far only a mother, a wood-shed, and four other soft, wobbly, black, hammer-headed angels, smelling of themselves, and warmth, and wood shavings. It was pleasant to feel that to us he would surrender an untouched love, that is, if he would surrender anything. Suppose he did not take to us!

And just then something must have stirred in him, for he turned up his swollen nose and stared at my companion, and a little later rubbed the dry pinkness of his tongue against my thumb. In that look, and that unconscious restless lick, he was trying hard to leave unhappiness behind, trying hard to feel that these new creatures with stroking paws and queer scents were his mother; yet all the time he knew, I am sure, that they were something bigger, more permanently, desperately, his. The first sense of being owned, perhaps (who knows) of owning, had stirred in him. He would never again be quite the same unconscious creature.

A little way from the end of our journey we got out and dismissed the cab. He could not too soon know the scents and pavements of this London where the chief of his life must pass. I can see now his first bumble down that wide, backwater of a street, how continually and suddenly he sat down to make sure of his own legs, how continually he lost our heels. He showed us then in full perfection what was afterwards to be an inconvenient—if endearing—characteristic: At any call or whistle he would look in precisely the opposite direction. How many times all through his life have I not seen him, at my whistle, start violently and turn his tail to me, then, with nose thrown searchingly from side to side, begin to canter toward the horizon!

In that first walk, we met, fortunately, but one vehicle, a brewer's dray; he chose that moment to attend to the more serious affairs of life, sitting quietly before the horses' feet and requiring to be moved by hand. From the beginning he had his dignity, and was extremely difficult to lift, owing to the length of his middle distance.

What strange feelings must have stirred in his little white soul when he first smelled carpet! But it was all so strange to him that day—I doubt if he felt more than I did when I first travelled to my private school, reading "Tales of a Grandfather," and plied with tracts and sherry by my father's man of business.

That night, indeed, for several nights, he slept with me, keeping me too warm down my back, and waking me now and then with quaint sleepy whimperings. Indeed, all through his life he flew a good deal in his sleep, fighting dogs and seeing ghosts, running after rabbits and thrown sticks; and to the last one never quite knew whether or no to rouse him when his four black feet began to jerk and quiver. His dreams were like our dreams, both good and bad; happy sometimes, sometimes tragic to weeping point.

He ceased to sleep with me the day we discovered that he was a perfect little colony, whose settlers were of an active species which I have never seen again. After that he had many beds, for circumstance ordained that his life should be nomadic, and it is to this I trace that philosophic indifference to place or property, which marked him out from most of his own kind. He learned early that for a black dog with long silky ears, a feathered tail, and head of great dignity, there was no home whatsoever, away from those creatures with special scents, who took liberties with his name, and alone of all created things were privileged to smack him with a slipper. He would sleep anywhere, so long as it was in their room, or so close outside it as to make no matter, for it was with him a principle that what he did not smell did not exist. I would I could hear again those long rubber-lipped snufflings of recognition underneath the door, with which each morning he would regale and reassure a spirit that grew with age more and more nervous and delicate about this matter of propinquity! For he was a dog of fixed ideas, things stamped on his mind were indelible; as, for example, his duty toward cats, for whom he had really a perverse affection, which had led to that first disastrous moment of his life, when he was brought up, poor bewildered puppy, from a brief excursion to the kitchen, with one eye closed and his cheek torn! He bore to his grave that jagged scratch across the eye. It was in dread of a repetition of this tragedy that he was instructed at the word "Cats" to rush forward with a special "tow-row-row-ing," which he never used toward any other form of creature. To the end he cherished a hope that he would reach the cat, but never did; and if he had, we knew he would only have stood and wagged his tail; but I well remember once, when he returned, important, from some such sally, how dreadfully my companion startled a cat-loving friend by murmuring in her most honeyed voice: "Well, my darling, have you been killing pussies in the garden?"

His eye and nose were impeccable in their sense of form; indeed, he was very English in that matter: People must be just so; things smell properly; and affairs go on in the one right way. He could tolerate neither creatures in ragged clothes, nor children on their hands and knees, nor postmen, because, with their bags, they swelled-up on one side, and carried lanterns on their stomachs. He would never let the harmless creatures pass without religious barks. Naturally a believer in authority and routine, and distrusting spiritual adventure, he yet had curious fads that seemed to have nested in him, quite outside of all principle. He would, for instance, follow neither carriages nor horses, and if we tried to make him, at once left for home, where he would sit with nose raised to Heaven, emitting through it a most lugubrious, shrill noise. Then again, one must not place a stick, a slipper, a glove, or anything with which he could play, upon one's head—since such an action reduced him at once to frenzy. For so conservative a dog, his environment was sadly anarchistic. He never complained in words of our shifting habits, but curled his head round over his left paw and pressed his chin very hard against the ground whenever he smelled packing. What necessity—he seemed continually to be saying—what real necessity is there for change of any kind whatever? Here we were all together, and one day was like another, so that I knew where I was—and now *you* only know what will happen next; and *I*—I can't tell you whether I shall be with you when it happens! What strange, grieving minutes a dog passes at such times in the underground of his subconsciousness, refusing realisation, yet all the time only too well divining. Some careless word, some unmuted compassion in voice, the stealthy wrapping of a pair of boots, the unaccustomed shutting of a door that ought to be open, the removal from a down-stair room of an object always there—one tiny thing, and he knows for certain that he is not going too. He fights against the knowledge just as we do against what we cannot bear; he gives up hope, but not effort, protesting in the only way he knows of, and now and then heaving a great sigh. Those sighs of a dog! They go to the heart so much more deeply than the sighs of our own kind, because they are utterly unintended, regardless of effect, emerging from one who, heaving them, knows not that they have escaped him!

The words: "Yes—going too!" spoken in a certain tone, would call up in his eyes a still-questioning half-happiness, and from his tail a quiet flutter, but did not quite serve to put to rest either his doubt or his feeling that it was all unnecessary—until the cab arrived. Then he would pour himself out of door or window, and be found in the bottom of the vehicle, looking severely away from an admiring cabman. Once settled on our feet he travelled with philosophy, but no digestion.

I think no dog was ever more indifferent to an outside

world of human creatures; yet few dogs have made more conquests—especially among strange women, through whom, however, he had a habit of looking—very discouraging. He had, natheless, one or two particular friends, and a few persons whom he knew he had seen before, but, broadly speaking, there were in his world of men, only his mistress, and—the almighty.

Each August, till he was six, he was sent for health, and the assuagement of his hereditary instincts, up to a Scotch shooting, where he carried many birds in a very tender manner. Once he was compelled by Fate to remain there nearly a year; and we went up ourselves to fetch him home. Down the long avenue toward the keeper's cottage we walked. It was high autumn; there had been frost already, for the ground was fine with red and yellow leaves; and presently we saw himself coming, professionally questing among those leaves, and preceding his dear keeper with the businesslike self-containment of a sportsman; not too fat, glossy as a raven's wing, swinging his ears and sporran like a little Highlander. We approached him silently. Suddenly his nose went up from its imagined trail, and he came rushing at our legs. From him, as a garment drops from a man, dropped all his strange soberness; he became in a single instant one fluttering eagerness. He leaped from life to life in one bound, without hesitation, without regret. Not one sigh, not one look back, not the faintest token of gratitude or regret at leaving those good people who had tended him for a whole year, buttered oat-cake for him, allowed him to choose each night exactly where he would sleep. No, he just marched out beside us, as close as ever he could get, drawing us on in spirit, and not even attending to the scents, until the lodge gates were passed.

It was strictly in accordance with the perversity of things, and something in the nature of calamity that he had not been ours one year, when there came over me a dreadful but overmastering aversion from killing those birds and creatures of which he was so fond as soon as they were dead. And so I never knew him as a sportsman; for during that first year he was only an unbroken puppy, tied to my waist for fear of accidents, and carefully pulling me off ev-

ery shot. They tell me he developed a lovely nose and perfect mouth, large enough to hold gingerly the biggest hare. I
well believe it, remembering the qualities of his mother,
whose character, however, in stability he far surpassed. But
as *he* grew every year more devoted to dead grouse and
birds and rabbits, *I* liked them more and more alive; it was
the only real breach between us, and we kept it out of sight.
Ah! well; it is consoling to reflect that I should infallibly
have ruined his sporting qualities, lacking that peculiar
habit of meaning what one says, so necessary to keep dogs
virtuous. But surely to have had him with me, quivering
and alert, with his solemn, eager face, would have given a
new joy to those crisp mornings when the hope of wings
coming to the gun makes poignant in the sportsman, as
nothing else will, an almost sensual love of Nature, a fierce
delight in the soft glow of leaves, in the white birch stems
and tracery of sparse twigs against blue sky, in the scents of
sap and grass and gum and heather flowers; stivers the hair
of him with keenness for interpreting each sound, and fills
the very fern or moss he kneels on, the very trunk he leans
against, with strange vibration.

Slowly Fate prepares for each of us the religion that lies
coiled in our most secret nerves; with such we cannot trifle,
we do not even try! But how shall a man grudge any one
sensations he has so keenly felt? Let such as have never
known those curious delights uphold the hand of horror—
for me there can be no such luxury. If I could, I would still
perhaps be knowing them; but when once the joy of life in
those winged and furry things has knocked at the very por-
tals of one's spirit, the thought that by pressing a little iron
twig one will rive that joy out of their vitals is too hard to
bear. Call it aestheticism, squeamishness, namby-pamby
sentimentalism, what you will—it is stronger than oneself!

Yes, after one had once watched with an eye that did not
merely see, the thirsty gaping of a slowly dying bird, or a
rabbit dragging a broken leg to a hole where he would lie for
hours thinking of the fern to which he should never more
come forth—after that, there was always the following little
matter of arithmetic: Given, that all those who had been
shooting were "good-fair" shots—which, Heaven knew, they

never were—they yet missed one at least in four, and did not miss it very much; so that if seventy-five things were slain, there were also twenty-five that had been fired at, and, of those twenty-five, twelve and a half had "gotten it" somewhere in their bodies, and would "likely" die at their great leisure.

This was the sum that brought about the only cleavage in our lives; and so, as he grew older, and trying to part from each other we no longer could, he ceased going to Scotland. But after that I often felt, and especially when we heard guns, how the best and most secret instincts of him were being stifled. But what was to be done? In that which was left of a clay pigeon he would take not the faintest interest —the scent of it was paltry. Yet always, even in his most cosseted and idle days, he managed to preserve the grave preoccupation of one professionally concerned with retrieving things that smell; and consoled himself with pastimes such as cricket, which he played in a manner highly specialised, following the ball up the moment it left the bowler's hand, and sometimes retrieving it before it reached the batsman. When remonstrated with, he would consider a little, hanging out a pink tongue and looking rather too eagerly at the ball, then canter slowly out to a sort of forward short leg. Why he always chose that particular position it is difficult to say; possibly he could lurk there better than anywhere else, the batsman's eye not being on him, and the bowler's not too much. As a fieldsman he was perfect, but for an occasional belief that he was not merely short leg, but slip, point, mid-off, and wicket-keep; and perhaps a tendency to make the ball a little "jubey." But he worked tremendously, watching every movement; for he knew the game thoroughly, and seldom delayed it more than three minutes when he secured the ball. And if that ball were really lost, then indeed he took over the proceedings with an intensity and quiet vigor that destroyed many shrubs, and the solemn satisfaction which comes from being in the very centre of the stage.

But his most passionate delight was swimming in anything except the sea, for which, with its unpleasant noise and habit of tasting salt, he had little affection. I see him now, cleaving the Serpentine, with his air of "the world well lost," striving to reach my stick before it had touched water. Being only a large spaniel, too small for mere heroism, he saved no lives in the water but his own—and that, on one occasion, before our very eyes, from a dark trout stream, which was trying to wash him down into a black hole among the boulders.

The call of the wild—Spring running—whatever it is—that besets men and dogs, seldom attained full mastery over him; but one could often see it struggling against his devotion to the scent of us, and, watching that dumb contest, I have time and again wondered how far this civilisation of ours was justifiably imposed on him; how far the love for us that we had so carefully implanted could ever replace in him the satisfaction of his primitive wild yearnings. He was like a man, naturally polygamous, married to one loved woman.

It was surely not for nothing that Rover is dog's most common name, and would be ours, but for our too tenacious fear of losing something, to admit, even to ourselves, that we are hankering. There was a man who said: Strange that two such queerly opposite qualities as courage and hypocrisy are the leading characteristics of the Anglo-Saxon! But is not hypocrisy just a product of tenacity, which is again the lower part of courage? Is not hypocrisy but an active sense of property in one's good name, the clutching close of respectability at any price, the feeling that one must not part, even at the cost of truth, with what he has sweated so to gain? And so we Anglo-Saxons will not answer to the name of Rover, and treat our dogs so that they, too, hardly know their natures.

The history of his one wandering, for which no respectable reason can be assigned, will never, of course, be known. It was in London, of an October evening, when we were told he had slipped out and was not anywhere. Then began those four distressful hours of searching for that black needle in that blacker bundle of hay. Hours of real dismay and suffering—for it is suffering, indeed, to feel a loved thing swallowed up in that hopeless maze of London streets. Stolen or run over? Which was worst? The neighboring police stations visited, the Dog's Home notified, an order for five hundred "Lost Dog" bills placed in the printer's hands, the streets patrolled! And then, in a lull snatched for food, and still endeavoring to preserve some aspect of assurance, we heard the bark which meant: "Here is a door I cannot open!" We hurried forth, and there he was on the top doorstep—busy, unashamed, giving no explanations, asking for his supper; and very shortly after him came his five hundred "Lost Dog" bills. Long I sat looking at him that night after my companion had gone up, thinking of the evening, some years before, when there followed us that shadow of a spaniel who had been lost for eleven days. And my heart turned over within me. But he! He was asleep, for he knew not remorse.

Ah! and there was that other time, when it was reported to me, returning home at night, that he had gone out to find me; and I went forth again, disturbed, and whistling his special call to the empty fields. Suddenly out of the darkness I heard a rushing, and he came furiously dashing against my heels for he alone knew where he had been lurking and saying to himself: I will not go in till he comes! I could not scold, there was something too lyrical in the return of that live, lonely, rushing piece of blackness through the blacker night. After all, the vagary was but a variation in his practice when one was away at bed-time, of passionately scratching up his bed in protest, till it resembled nothing; for, in spite of his long and solemn face and the silkiness of his ears, there was much in him yet of the cave bear —he dug graves on the smallest provocations, in which he never buried anything. He was not a "clever" dog; and guiltless of all tricks. Nor was he ever "shown." We did not even dream of subjecting him to this indignity. Was our dog a clown, a hobby, a fad, a fashion, a feather in our caps—that we should subject him to periodic pennings in stuffy halls, that we should harry his faithful soul with such tomfoolery? He never even heard us talk about his lineage, deplore the length of his nose, or call him "clever-looking." We should have been ashamed to let him smell about us the tar-brush of a sense of property, to let him think we looked on him as an asset to earn us pelf or glory. We wished that there should be between us the spirit that was between the sheep-dog and that farmer, who, when asked his dog's age, touched the old creature's head, and answered thus: "Teresa" (his daughter) "was born in November, and this one in August." That sheep-dog had seen eighteen years when the great white day came for him, and his spirit passed away up, to cling with the wood-smoke round the dark rafters of the kitchen where he had lain so vast a time beside his master's boots. No, no! If a man does not soon pass beyond the thought: "By what shall this dog profit me?" into the large state of simple gladness to be with dog, he shall never know the very essence of that companionship which depends not on the points of dog, but on some strange and subtle mingling of mute spirits. For it is by muteness that a dog becomes for one so utterly beyond value; with him one is at peace, where words play no torturing tricks. When he just sits, loving, and knows that he is being loved, those are the moments that I think are precious to a dog; when, with his adoring soul coming through his eyes, he feels that you are really thinking of him. But he is touchingly tolerant of one's other occupations. The subject of these memories always knew when one was too absorbed in work to be so close to him as he thought proper; yet he never tried to hinder or distract, or asked for attention. It dinged his mood, of course, so that the red under his eyes and the folds of his crumply cheeks—which seemed to speak of a touch of bloodhound introduced a long way back into his breeding—grew deeper and more manifest. If he could have spoken at such times, he would have said: "I have been a long time alone, and I cannot always be asleep; but you know best, and I must not criticise."

He did not at all mind one's being absorbed in other humans; he seemed to enjoy the sounds of conversation lifting round him, and to know when they were sensible. He could not, for instance, stand actors or actresses giving readings of their parts, perceiving at once that the same had no connection with the minds and real feelings of the speakers; and, having wandered a little to show his disapproval, he would go to the door and stare at it till it opened and let him out. Once or twice, it is true, when an actor of large voice was declaiming an emotional passage, he so far relented as to go up to him and pant in his face. Music, too, made him restless, inclined to sigh, and to ask questions. Sometimes, at its first sound, he would cross to the window and remain there looking for Her. At others, he would simply go and lie on the loud pedal, and we never could tell whether it was from sentiment, or because he thought that in this way he heard less. At one special Nocturne of Chopin's he always whimpered. He *was,* indeed, of rather Polish temperament —very gay when he was gay, dark and brooding when he was not.

On the whole, perhaps his life was uneventful for so far-travelling a dog, though it held its moments of eccentricity, as when he leaped through the window of a four-wheeler into Kensington, or sat on a Dartmoor adder. But that was fortunately of a Sunday afternoon—when adder and all were torpid, so nothing happened, till a friend, who was following, lifted him off the creature with his large boot.

If only one could have known more of his private life— more of his relations with his own kind! I fancy he was always rather a dark dog to them, having so many thoughts about us that he could not share with any one, and being naturally fastidious, except with ladies, for whom he had a chivalrous and catholic taste, so that they often turned and snapped at him. He had, however, but one lasting love affair, for a liver-colored lass of our village, not quite of his own caste, but a wholesome if somewhat elderly girl, with loving and sphinx-like eyes. Their children, alas, were not for this world, and soon departed.

Nor was he a fighting dog; but once attacked, he lacked a sense of values, being unable to distinguish between dogs that he could beat and dogs with whom he had "no earthly." It was, in fact, as well to interfere at once, especially in the matter of retrievers, for he never forgot having in his youth been attacked by a retriever from behind. No, he never forgot, and never forgave, an enemy. Only a month before that day of which I cannot speak, being very old and ill, he engaged an Irish terrier on whose impudence he had long had his eye, and routed him. And how a battle cheered his spirit! He was certainly no Christian; but, allowing for essential dog, he was very much a gentleman. And I do think that most of us who live on this earth these days would rather leave it with that label on us than the other. For to be a Christian, as Tolstoy understood the word—and no one else in our time has had logic and love of truth enough to give it coherent meaning—is (to be quite sincere) not suited to men of Western blood. Whereas—to be a gentleman! It is a far cry, but perhaps it can be done. In him, at all events, there was no pettiness, no meanness, and no cruelty, and though he fell below his ideal at times, this never altered the true look of his eyes, nor the simple loyalty in his soul.

But what a crowd of memories come back, bringing with them the perfume of fallen days! What delights and glamour, what long hours of effort, discouragements, and secret fears did he not watch over—our black familiar; and with the sight and scent and touch of him, deepen or assuage! How many thousand walks did we not go together, so that we still turn to see if he is following at his padding gait, attentive to the invisible trails. Not the least hard thing to bear when they go from us, these quiet friends, is that they carry away with them so many years of our own lives. Yet, if they find warmth therein, who would grudge them those years that they have so guarded? Nothing else of us can they take to lie upon with outstretched paws and chin pressed to the ground; and, whatever they take, be sure they have deserved.

Do they know, as we do, that their time must come? Yes, they know, at rare moments. No other way can I interpret those pauses of his latter life, when, propped on his forefeet, he would sit for long minutes quite motionless—his head drooped, utterly withdrawn; then turn those eyes of his and look at me. That look said more plainly than all words could: "Yes, I know that I must go!" If *we* have spirits that persist—*they* have. If *we* know, after our departure, who we were—*they* do. No one, I think, who really longs for truth, can ever glibly say which it will be for dog and man—persistence or extinction of our consciousness. There is but one thing certain—the childishness of fretting over that eternal question. Whichever it be, it must be right, the only possible thing. He felt that too, I know; but then, like his master, he was what is called a pessimist.

My companion tells me that, since he left us, he has once come back. It was Old Year's Night, and she was sad, when he came to her in visible shape of his black body, passing round the dining-table from the window-end, to his proper place beneath the table, at her feet. She saw him quite clearly; she heard the padding tap-tap of his paws and very toe-nails; she felt his warmth brushing hard against the front of her skirt. She thought then that he would settle down upon her feet, but something disturbed him, and he stood pausing, pressed against her, then moved out toward where I generally sit, but was not sitting that night. She saw him stand there, as if considering; then at some sound or laugh, she became self-conscious, and slowly, very slowly, he was no longer there. Had he some message, some counsel to give, something he would say, that last night of the last year of all those he had watched over us? Will he come back again?

No stone stands over where he lies. It is on our hearts that his life is engraved.

Stanley Bing

THE MOST BEAUTIFUL GIRL IN THE WORLD

It was the last autumn of innocence, I think. Boston was green and gold and all kinds of bright orange, vermilion, and paisley, the air so crisp and fresh, and all things were possible. The Sox had just won the sixth game of the best World Series ever. Nixon had been gone for a year; drugs were still as American as scrapple; sex was safer than it would ever be again, at least physically. I was standing on the platform of the Red Line with my soon-to-be-ex-fiancée, Doris, who was bothering me about something, as she did between 1972 and 1976. It was early evening. Down at the end of the station sat a midsize ersatz collie dog, just beyond puppyhood, laughing. Her eyes glowed with a tremendous good nature and trust unencumbered by a surfeit of complicated insights. She was alone.

"Hi," I said. She came over, licked my hand discreetly, allowed herself to be scratched for a time, chased her tail in a dignified circle, lay down again. I remember thinking: "There are times God puts a choice in front of you." I often had such thoughts back then.

We took the dog.

She went totally nuts when she understood the news, bounding and leaping in a vertical parabola to kiss my face, and generally expressing an exuberance that made me want to laugh. As a world view, it was so inappropriate. Searching for the makings of a proto-leash, Doris found in her bottomless denim bag a hank of purple yarn, possibly the one she used for the three-year Sweater for Stan Project, the completion of which turned out to signify the end of our relationship. I wrapped several lengths around her neck—the dog's, that is—but it did not serve. To get her home in one piece, I had to pick her up and hold her like a baby. It is a silly position for a dog, and most fight it. Not her. She lay in my arms, feet poking skyward, head lolling back in a friendly grin, tongue draping out of the corner of her mouth, eyes calmly investigating mine as if to say, "Hey, this is a nice idea. Why didn't you think of it before?"

At the time, I made $8,000 a year. My car was a pre-Nissan Datsun, basically a floorboard with wheels and perforated tin skin. My diet consisted of doughnuts, peanut butter, and Chef Boyardee ravioli straight from the can. Cold. My rent was $155 a month for six rooms. The sink was piled to eye level with every dish in the house, since Doris and I also couldn't get together on the politics of kitchen work.

I named the dog Elizabeth. Height: about thirty inches. Weight: thirty-five pounds. Eyes: brown. Tongue: red. Tail: rich and plumy. A coat of pure china white, so thick and lustrous and profuse that people would later suggest that I shear her and turn the output into a serape. In the summer she shed badly. In the winter, worse. All my clothes and furniture were coated with a fine layer of white flax. When she was young, her tummy was as pink as a baby's bottom, and she had a marvelous doggy smell, clean, pungent, yet sweet. Her personality? All I can say is that when the Lord made her, he forgot to add any malice, guile, or aggressiveness. Didn't chase squirrels, even. If another dog attacked her, she would roll over on her back immediately and expose her soft underbelly, clearly conveying the message: "Go ahead and kill me. I don't mind, but I think it would be a totally unnecessary waste of energy. But hey, just my opinion." Not once in her life was she hurt by any living creature.

Elizabeth was not smart, but she made the most of it.

"She's the sweetest dog in the world," said a friend about her. "But she's got an IQ somewhere between a brick and a houseplant." When people asked what breed she was, we'd say, "Mexican Brainless." How we'd laugh! In retrospect, this seems kind of unfair. Could she defend her thoughts, assuming she had any? Not at all. For all intents and purposes, she was mute: Not a bark, yelp, or whimper escaped her. In fourteen years, I heard her voice maybe three times. It was always a shock.

I broke up with Doris and rented a place that was nice before I got to it. I was not a master of business administration then, and it was not the living space of a responsible person. Many was the night Liz and I stayed up until dawn, eating biscuits and watching Charlie Chan. Her nose was big and black and wet and perfect for squeezing, and she liked nothing better than to sit at my side and lick my hand for hours on end. I think she got into a kind of trance when she did it, and I had to slap her around now and then to get her to stop.

No roommate could have suited me better. One afternoon, looking under my bed for a shoe to munch, she found a blue sphere covered with a gossamer pelt of fuzz. It had been an orange once, but now it was soft and alien to the touch. Any sensible person would have tossed it out immediately. I found her playing with it. Took a hell of a chase to get it away from her too.

Not long after, when the nation was spritzing its bicentennial all over itself, I met my soon-to-be future wife. Before long we were sort of living together. Dogs were not welcome in her building, so Elizabeth was forced to hold down the fort at my apartment. After a while, it became a dog's apartment, which I guess was only fair. Empty cans of her Alpo and my ravioli littered the rooms, and long skeins of toilet paper hung everywhere, for when Liz got bored, she loved to play with it, string it out, flip it over and under things. She tore into Hefty bags and distributed the contents. She kept herself occupied.

She also periodically ran away. If you opened a door or window, she was out it. One morning she tore through a screen and hurled herself to the street. I didn't blame her.

The place was a pit. It was a good thing I lived on the ground floor.

She loved to run, that was it. I would take her to a nearby football field once every couple of days. It was fenced in. I'd let her off the leash, and she would sprint in an immense circle around the huge enclosure until I thought her heart would pop from exertion and joy. Then I'd pile her in the back of the car, where she'd sleep, heaving up and down as she dreamt, and shed. That was fine with me. It was a dog's car, too.

We got married, my wife and I, and for a while there Elizabeth was our only child. She got a lot of love. After a year, we moved to the city, and she, like us, learned to adjust to the demands of urban living. When we'd return home from a walk, I'd let her off the leash in the long hallway down to our three-room flat, and she'd tear down that corridor like a hound possessed, her tail tucked underneath her rear end for maximum aerodynamic lift and thrust, slam into the wall at the end, turn, and head back at even greater speed.

She was youth, and spirit, and dumb, careless vitality.

We were city people now, with city rituals. When we went to the mandatory summer community to visit friends, she was there, zipping freely down the beach in those days before the invention of deer ticks, chasing the waves until they crashed over her and I had to rescue her from the undertow. One night, we went back to eat sesame noodles and chicken, and our hostess put the salad on the floor since the table was full unto groaning. In the candlelight, as we talked, we heard a moist chomping sound, and a great smacking of lips. We looked underneath the table, and it was Liz, downing the last of the arugula and goat cheese and sun-dried tomatoes. She looked up at us, the vinaigrette glistening off her whiskers, as if to say, "Gosh, this is delicious, guys, but not that filling. How about some chicken bones to wash it down?"

To her, carcass of used poultry was the ultimate delicacy. One time, I left an entire oven-stuffer roaster wrapped in tinfoil on the kitchen counter. Two hours later, the only thing left in the room was a small piece of tinfoil and a grease spot on the floor. She had eaten not only the meat and bones, but the aluminum as well. I watched her for days, certain she had finally OD'd on her own sheer witlessness. But she hadn't.

She was indestructible.

She took the birth of our two kids with grace, even when they pulled her eyebrows or fell on her screaming and hugging and kissing her with the kind of passion adults usually reserve for the game-show hosts who award them cruises to Bimini. When my son was a year old, and particularly aggressive, he tried to ride her. She was thirteen by then, and growled at him. After some thought, it was determined that it was she who would be sent away to stay at my mother's house. The exile lasted six weeks. She went with the program after that.

One morning in 1988, she couldn't get up. I took her to the vet, who told me that her spleen was enlarged. Would I care to make a decision? After all, the dog was fourteen. We fixed her up. It was the best money I ever spent, and I spent a lot of it. While she was convalescing at the hospital, my son put together his first complete sentence: "I miss Wizbet," he said. And then he cried. How much is a dog's life worth?

Last winter we moved to a house with a backyard, a swing, and a piece of an acre. Elizabeth came, too.

So a month ago my wife and children went down to see my in-laws in Arizona. And the following Thursday, after breakfast, Liz fell down in the garden and just lay there, her eyes rolled up into her skull, heaving and panting and trembling. The episode lasted just a few minutes, but it scared me shitless. When she awoke, she was jolly and hungry, and spent the rest of the day in the backyard, staring off into space, always one of her favorite pastimes.

When she was falling down five times a day, the vet said to me, "You have to decide whether she is able to preserve her dignity leading this type of existence." I'd never considered it in those terms before. As she lay on her side, clearly not in the world as we know it, I held her paw and kissed her forehead, and all the fourteen years of my life with her swam before me and I knew, yes I did. And it was not a good knowing. I made a call. I put her in the car. My brother came along. We were both crying.

The vet's office was clean and cool. He's a nice guy, my vet. I got the feeling that he'd never get used to that part of his job. "This shot will put her to sleep easily," he said. "Then the next shot will put her to rest." He gave her the first and suddenly she arched her back and from her throat came a horrible, gut-wrenching cry, a raking, moaning howl that conveyed an understanding nobody needs to have, and for which none of us is ever ready. And my brother and I held her, and we were sobbing, and the vet said, "She's not in pain, she's just had a neurological reaction to the sedative." Then a few minutes later: "She's at peace." He was weeping, too.

Her body was there, the coat still shiny, the nose still wet and warm. But *she* was gone. I noticed a small pulse in the tip of her tongue, which was hanging out of her mouth much as it had the very first night I saw her, in October of 1975, when Pete Rose was a hero and Boston was nine innings away from its first world championship in nearly six decades.

This is the last I will speak of her. I owe her this eulogy, dog to dog, for fourteen years of companionship, of laughs and devotion and cheek-by-jowl existence on this hard and incomprehensible planet.

E. B. White

OBITUARY

Daisy ("Black Watch Debatable") died December 22, 1931, when she was hit by a Yellow Cab in University Place. At the moment of her death she was smelling the front of a florist's shop. It was a wet day, and the cab skidded up over the curb—just the sort of excitement that would have amused her, had she been at a safer distance. She is survived by her mother, Jeannie; a brother, Abner; her father, whom she never knew; and two sisters, whom she never liked. She was three years old.

Daisy was born at 65 West Eleventh Street in a clothes closet at two o'clock of a December morning in 1928. She came, as did her sisters and brothers, as an unqualified surprise to her mother, who had for several days previously looked with a low-grade suspicion on the box of bedding that had been set out for the delivery, and who had gone into the clothes closet merely because she had felt funny and wanted a dark, awkward place to feel funny in. Daisy was the smallest of the litter of seven, and the oddest.

Her life was full of incident but not of accomplishment. Persons who knew her only slightly regarded her as an opinionated little bitch, and said so; but she had a small circle of friends who saw through her, cost what it did. At Speyer Hospital, where she used to go when she was indisposed, she was known as "Whitey," because, the man told me, she was black. All her life she was subject to moods, and her feeling about horses laid her sanity open to question. Once she slipped her leash and chased a horse for three blocks through heavy traffic, in the carking belief that she was an effective agent against horses. Drivers of teams, seeing her only in the moments of her delirium, invariably leaned far out of their seats and gave tongue, mocking her; and thus made themselves even more ridiculous, for the moment, than Daisy.

She had a stoical nature, and spent the latter part of her life an invalid, owing to an injury to her right hind leg. Like many invalids, she developed a rather objectionable cheerfulness, as though to deny that she had cause for rancor. She also developed, without instruction or encouragement, a curious habit of holding people firmly by the ankle without actually biting them—a habit that gave her an immense personal advantage and won her many enemies. As far as I know, she never even broke the thread of a sock, so delicate was her grasp (like a retriever's), but her point of view was questionable, and her attitude was beyond explaining to the person whose ankle was at stake. For my own amusement, I often tried to diagnose this quirkish temper, and I think I understand it: she suffered from a chronic perplexity, and it relieved her to take hold of something.

She was arrested once, by Patrolman Porko. She enjoyed practically everything in life except motoring, an exigency to which she submitted silently, without joy, and without nausea. She never took pains to discover, conclusively, the things that might have diminished her curiosity and spoiled her taste. She died sniffing life, and enjoying it.

Ross Santee

WRINKLE AND I

The pup was asleep. His warm bed was in a shallow box behind the kitchen stove, beside the box was a pan of clean ashes for the puppy's needs. While Mother was always a gentle person, she could be firm; when Mother housebroke a puppy or kitten there was no piddling or puddling about the house. And the pup was a surprise.

Of course, I could hold him for he was mine. He grunted, still half asleep, when I picked him up. He didn't smell like a kitten when I held him against my neck; Mother said puppies had a smell of their own the same as kittens. And what would I call him? I didn't know, but he looked kind of wrinkled to me. "That might be a good name," suggested Mother, "if it pleases you." And so we called him Wrinkle.

I was not allowed to hold him when I ate, but he was asleep in my arms when the second bell rang for school. "Now, heel it, son," Mother said, "or you'll be late. He'll be here when you get home."

At recess I told Bert Phillips about him, Bert was my first friend. When school let out Bert and I raced all the way. Wrinkle was asleep, but I carried him outside and put him down on the wooden sidewalk. Like all pups he spraddled out for it was a big, strange and new world to him but he did his best to please. When I spoke he tried to come to me; he finally took a header off the walk that was all of eight inches high and landed in a pile of autumn leaves. I picked him up and let Bert hold him, and my friend agreed that he was the finest pup that ever lived.

Someone suggested that if I wanted to make a good "ratter" out of him that I put the pup in a box with a rat and let them have it out. I was too small to realize how cruel it was, but it seemed like a good idea at the time. The wire trap in the corn crib at the barn often held more than a dozen sizable rats when I inspected it in the morning. One of the first chores that I recall was dumping the trap into a half barrel of water and dispatching the vermin that way.

I took a large tight packing box from the kindling yard, one deep enough that I didn't think a rat could scale the sides. But as a precaution I kept a broomstick handy. After taking such precautions I put Wrinkle in with him. He was still a puppy, still had his puppy teeth, and not much bigger than the rat he had been called to do battle with. Wrinkle knew it wasn't another puppy or a kitten, but he was perfectly willing to play.

It wasn't until the rat bit him and the puppy squealed that I realized what a cruel thing I'd done. I couldn't use the broomstick for fear of hitting the pup. And he was a fuzzy ball of fury now. Aside from the first squeal, the only sound the puppy made was a little throaty growl; it was the rat that did the squealing as they raged about the box. Wrinkle knew the fight was to the death and he was game to the core.

Mother finally heard me crying and cussing from the house, and knowing I was in trouble she appeared upon the scene. For I was in the box with them when Wrinkle laid him low. Even with the dead rat he still raged like a little fury. It was Mother who picked him out of the box and examined the puppy's wounds. "Of course, you didn't know any better," she said, "but you won't do it again. What a gritty little fellow he is." It wasn't until we reached the house that Mother discovered the rat had also bitten me. But Mother not only had a green thumb when it came to growing things, her hands were healing too.

He grew into a clean-bodied, clean-legged black and tan terrier, and we were inseparable. When he was big enough to follow he was always at my heels. Older boys and grown men too thought it amusing the way he'd snap and bite when they made a pass at me. But it wasn't so amusing when he lost his puppy teeth. And while he tolerated the neighbors he was never a friendly dog, and the sight of a stranger passing our house would always touch him off.

We had gone uptown on an errand for Mother. There was a group of men at the hitching rack at Seymour's General Store. We were passing the rack when the stranger spoke, a farm hand I'd never seen before. "There's that feist that run out an' bit me when I passed the house." As he spoke, the man pulled up his overalls. He wore no socks. It was obvious that he had come from the fields for his leg was dirty. The teeth marks were obvious too.

Now a small boy might take a personal insult from a grown man but it is always advisable to let his dog alone. "He's not a feist," I said, "for he's my dog." In the meantime Wrinkle, thinking it was the usual game, planted himself firmly between us, emitting throaty growls the while and showing his fine strong teeth.

The farm hand spoke again, "You're feisty, too, for so small a brat." As he spoke he aimed a kick at the dog. But it was an old game to Wrinkle and the little dog was quick. In the hassle that followed the farm hand was bitten again. Wrinkle and I both heeled it then. And on our return from our errand, as a matter of discretion, we passed the rack on the opposite side of the street.

We hunted rabbits that winter without success for we were both pretty small. When the snow was deep I carried him. Armed with a broomstick the pup and I worked every brush pile we could find. As for our winter's hunting we had more success at the barns for a rat was Wrinkle's mortal enemy until the day he died. And while Iowa boasted of its corn, it was rat-heaven for the vermin.

At the word "rats" Wrinkle would go into a tizzy. Mother finally forbade me saying the word in the house for at any mention of the word he would take the place apart. In bad weather we spent hours at the barns together; while I prodded and poked in odd places with the broomstick, Wrinkle dispatched the vermin when they came into the open. The hands at Lucas' farm next door often helped with the aid of a three-tined fork.

Dan Lucas, a neighbor, had holdings in the Northwest. It was not unusual for a trainload of Longhorns to be unloaded in our little town and the cowhands who accompanied them often wintered next door. They were eager participants too in what they called the "rat killin'" that we held most every morning. And like most cowhands I have known, a wager no matter how small was meat and drink to them.

For no longer did I dump the rat trap in the half barrel of water; the extermination of the vermin fell to Wrinkle, and how he enjoyed that chore. As long as one rat was dumped from the trap at a time I would wager a penny that no vermin could escape. Nor do I recall ever losing. But occasionally the hands made bets among themselves. When several rats were released from the trap at once some were bound to escape for Wrinkle never turned one loose until he was as dead as the proverbial door nail.

And of all Lucas' hands that I recall two are long-remembered. It could be the fact that they treated me as an equal and neither ever teased me nor did they tease my dog. One was John Scott and the other was Bert Morrison. Mother let me go any place with them.

John had gone to the pond to cut ice so the steers could water out. It was during the Xmas holidays and zero weather. Mother had bundled me so tight I had trouble moving about. I carried the pup in my arms. We were ready to leave when a big steer got on the prod. When he charged the empty rack I held on to the pup as best I could for I thought we were going over.

"Take it easy," said John, "if he tries it again I'll drop him." John had a .44 Winchester in the rack. He pumped a shell into the barrel and when the big steer charged the rack the second time John not only dropped him in his tracks, he got down and butchered the critter. He gave me the bladder as a souvenir and blew it up for me.

But it was too cold to play outside. After I'd kicked it about in the house for a time the bladder finally disappeared, and I always suspected Mother.

Bert Morrison was a cowboy. Years later when I read "The Virginian," that character—the tall black-headed guy —to me was always Bert. Wrinkle and I were always at his heels when he was on the ground. And the "long" rides to the Lucas' feed barns to the south and west were special occasions for the barns were more than a half mile from town. I'd gather Wrinkle in my arms, then Bert would swing me up in front. Nor was he ever one to ask a pony's permission as to whether he liked it or not.

There was one ride I recall where Wrinkle got all the worst of it. I had him in my arms when Bert swung me up in front. The pony went to pitching then and somewhere along the line I dropped my pup. That ride was rough; at times I dangled most precariously, but Bert still held me in an ample paw when the pony's head came up. I was afraid the pony might kick the pup if he tried to follow and the idea of leaving Wrinkle behind was the last thing on my mind. Bert was agreeable; when he swung me up in front the second time I managed to hold the pup, and with Bert holding me we finally rode out the storm.

My friends and I occasionally tried damming up the creek as a swimming pool, but seldom with any success; the dam usually went out on us before the water was belly-deep. It was much simpler to go to the railroad pond on the other side of town, and while the pond was off limits for me I learned to swim that summer.

There were usually older boys at the pond who took delight in throwing small fry into deep water, wetting clothes and tying them in knots. Since Wrinkle always guarded my clothes I was seldom molested. At any movement toward me there was usually a warning shouted, "You better lay off that one unless you want to get dog-bit!"

It was late summer. We had moved Wrinkle's bed out on the porch where he always waited for me when I opened the kitchen door. Then the morning came when he couldn't get out of his bed. Mother was afraid it was poison. I had never heard of a veterinary for there was none in our little town, but I ran for Dr. Hamilton, the family physician. His team and buggy was at the rack; he was just ready to make some early calls in the country when I barged into his office above the general store.

"What is it, Lengthy?" he said.

"Doctor, my dog is sick. He's awful sick."

The doctor spoke in his quiet voice, "We'll go and look at him right now."

We went to the house where he examined the dog. It was poison, he said, and since Mother had already done the right things there was nothing more he could do. When I searched his face for a ray of hope the doctor shook his head. "No, Lengthy," he said, "he's a pretty sick little dog."

I was shocked when Mother apologized for me fetching him—Wrinkle was as much a part of the family to me as my mother and sisters. And I recall the good doctor's reply, "It's quite all right; I understand how Lengthy feels for after all I have three boys of my own."

The days dragged on and they were interminable. I sat by the bed on the porch. Mother sent me on long errands of no point that I could see; instead of dawdling as was my usual custom I ran the errands both ways. Mother was hopeful too. When she finally insisted I go to bed that night I thought he might pull through.

It was breaking light next morning when I went to his bed on the porch. At first glance he might have been asleep as he often slept on his back—then I saw the distorted face. Mother dressed and hurried out when she heard me crying and cussing, for I knew all the barnyard words. And Mother was shocked when I said that as soon as I got big enough I'd kill whoever did it.

"Don't say such things!" she said. "Don't even think such things." Mother covered him with one of his blankets. She spoke of my father who had died when I was only a few months old. "You were too small to remember him. This is your first real hurt."

I dug the grave by an apple tree under Mother's supervision and got by pretty well until Mother carried him from his bed wrapped in his little blanket. I heeled it then for the big ragweed thicket by the slaughter house. Wrinkle and I always went there when I wanted to be alone. It was hours later when I returned. Nor did Mother insist that I eat, she understood why I went to bed without supper that night.

The dog had bitten many people, yet there were only two suspects as far as I was concerned. One was the big lout who had threatened to cut off my ample ears, the other was the farm hand. When I asked my friend Bert Morrison to shoot either one or both men for me Bert was almost as shocked as Mother. "Listen, kid," he said, "you can't go around shootin' folks whether they need it or not. But if I find out who did it I'll work him over for you."

Since my friend Bert had let me down I took things in hand myself. But when I faced the big lout I didn't get far with him; he not only stoutly denied it, he called me a "damn little wild cat."

The farm hand was at the rack by the hardware store with a group of men days later when I finally located him. I was crying when I faced him but they were tears of rage. "You killed my dog—you poisoned him—and I hope the lightning strikes you!"

The farm hand slowly shook his head and his were kindly eyes. "No, kid," he said. "He bit me; fact is, he bit me twicet. I tried to kick him too, but I wouldn't do a lousy thing like that. I lost the first dog I ever owned that way, somebody poisoned him. I'm sorry about your little dog for I know how you feel."

I was always somewhat dubious about the big lout; but as for the farm hand with the kindly eyes, I knew he spoke the truth.

John Updike

DOG'S DEATH

She must have been kicked unseen or brushed by a car.
Too young to know much, she was beginning to learn
To use the newspapers spread on the kitchen floor
And to win, wetting there, the words, "Good dog!
                                    Good dog!"

We thought her shy malaise was a shot reaction.
The autopsy disclosed a rupture in her liver.
As we teased her with play, blood was filling her skin
And her heart was learning to lie down forever.

Monday morning, as the children were noisily fed
And sent to school, she crawled beneath the youngest's
    bed.
We found her twisted and limp but still alive.
In the car to the vet's, on my lap, she tried

To bite my hand and died. I stroked her warm fur
And my wife called in a voice imperious with tears.
Though surrounded by love that would have upheld her,
Nevertheless she sank and, stiffening, disappeared.

Back home, we found that in the night her frame,
Drawing near to dissolution, had endured the shame
Of diarrhoea and had dragged across the floor
To a newspaper carelessly left there. *Good dog.*

John Burroughs

RECALLING SOME DOGS

Sept. 4, 1875. Reb is dead, and it seems as if a chapter in my life had closed. We buried him this morning by the rock near the path to the spring, where we shall pass and repass in all our farm work, and where the poor dog can hear the footfalls of the horse he loved so well.

I may live to be an old man, but I shall not live long enough to forget Reb. There was nothing between my heart and his; he was wholly within the circle of my most private affection; he touched me warm and close. I do not know in what way I should have loved a child differently—more deeply, perhaps, but not more genuinely. If my love for Reb was not the precious gold of the heart, it certainly was the silvered. In my younger days I should have thought less of him, but next to the members of my own family, Death could not have singled out an object half so precious and necessary to me. So great is my need of a comrade (within weeks Burroughs acquired Rover, later renamed Rosemary Rose), an untalking companion, on my walks, or boating, or about the farm; and, next to one's bosom friend, what companion like a dog? Your thought is his thought, your wish is his wish, and where you desire to go, that place of all others is preferable to him. It was bliss enough for Reb to be with me, and it was a never failing source of pleasure for me to be with Reb. Why should my grief be so acute? Only a dog.

My neighbor, or my friend, dies, or my man-servant, or maid-servant, who has served me long, and my grief is less poignant. My dog is a part of myself. He has no separate or individual existence; he lives wholly in and for me. But my friend, or my neighbor, revolves in an orbit of his own. He has his own schemes and purposes, and touches me only casually, or not clearly at all. My dog is interested in everything I do. Then he represents the spirit of holiday, of fun, of adventure. The world is still full of wonders to him, and in a journey of a mile, he has many adventures. Every journey is an excursion, a sally into an unknown land, teeming with curiosities. A dog lives only ten or fifteen years, but think how much he crowds into that space, how much energy and vitality he lives up.

Aug. 5, 1877. My beloved dog, Rosemary Rose, died this morning from poisoning. I do not need to write in my diary to remember it. It is burnt into my heart . . . Oh, a bitter day. None may know what that dog was to me. He and Reb were my children and my only comrades. I am quite desolate . . . We dug his grave this afternoon—Aaron and I— but tonight he lies in his bed at the foot of the stairs for the last time.

(Ten days after Rosemary Rose's death Burroughs got Lark. Both Lark, in August of 1881, and Laddie, on March 5, 1888, died after being bitten by a Newfoundland.)

Sept. 30, 1881. One's pleasure with a dog is unmixed. There are no setbacks. They make no demands upon you, as does a child; no care, no interruption, no intrusion. If you are busy, or want to sleep, or read, or be with your friend, they are as if they were not. When you want them, there they are at your elbow and ready for any enterprise. And the measure of your love they always return heaped up. Ah, well! I cannot but mourn—my daily companion and comrade (Lark) is gone. The door that opens and shuts but once, to dogs as well as to men, has closed behind him, and I shall see him no more, no more.

* * *

Dec. 23, 1889. My dog, I-Know, is dead—killed Friday night by the gravel train, as he tried to pass under it . . . I am less grieved than when my other dogs have died, because I have had experience and will not be caught that way again —will not allow a dog to take such a deep hold upon my affections. After a time, I suppose, I can lose dogs without emotion. But how I shall miss that faithful creature from my solitary life; and how long will his memory be fresh in my heart?

Autumn 1898. I make my last entry this month to record the death of my beloved dog, Nip, which occurred yesterday afternoon by his falling through the high railroad bridge over Black Creek. We went on a walk up the track, as we have done a hundred times. I heard a train coming down the track and called him back. He came to near the end, when he paused, and in some way his hind feet slipped off the tie and he fell through before my eyes. He struck heavily on the soft ground, got up and ran, crying a few yards, and fell in his death agony. When I got to him he had ceased to breathe.

It is one of the worst shocks I ever had and quite stunned me. For a moment the whole universe seemed bereft, and my whole outlook upon life changed.

I laid his limp body beside the abutment of the bridge and came home and passed a wretched night. When I was not thinking of him, I was dreaming of him. I dreamed of sending two girls for his body with a pole to which they were to tie it. I got the strings and pole for them. Then I dreamed that the railroad men had buried him, and had shot him before doing so; and Mrs. B guided me to the spot, and I dug him up.

This morning I brought him over here (Burroughs' 1887–1900 residence at Slabsides) in a basket and laid him down once more beside the fire, that my eyes might behold him again in his old place (just as he had done 21 years before with Rosemary Rose). What a counterfeit of sleep!

I did not know I loved the dog so. Now Hiram (Burroughs' brother) is gone, Nip was my only companion—almost a part of myself. (Nip was a fox terrier with a short tail, white with a black spot over one eye and ear.)

Nov. 1, 1898. I spend part of the day at Slabsides, trying to write, the thought of Nip constantly hovering about my mind. Men of my temperament make much of their griefs. It is another form of self-indulgence. We roll the bitter morsel under our tongues and extract the last drop of bitterness. It is probable that I make the death of Nip the occasion to gloat over the past, and that which can never return. This is my disease; it is in my system, and the loss of the dog brings it out afresh. It gives it an acute form. But I was deeply attached to him, and the thought of him will always be precious to me.

Nov. 2, 1898. Of all the domestic animals none calls forth so much love, solicitude, and sorrow as the dog. He occupies the middle place between the other animals and man. Our love for him is below that for our fellows, and above that we have for any other dumb creature. How many men there are now in the world, millions of them, whose love for their dogs is next to that they have for their friends and families! and their grief at their loss, next to a domestic bereavement!

Molly Ivins

WHAT'S IN A NAME?

Shit the Dog finally croaked on December 9 after fourteen-and-a-half years of marplotting through life. Shit was the *Texas Observer's* office dog in the early 1970s and, as such, did a lot to hold down the circulation of the magazine. Many who knew Shit consider her possibly the most worthless dog that ever lived, but they overlook her great talent—Shit had a genius for fouling things up.

As *Observer* dog, it was her invariable habit to greet all our readers who had faithfully climbed up three flights of stairs in order to renew their subscriptions by growling and snapping at them. Whereas, whenever some nut arrived at the office to scream about the communist propaganda we were publishing, she would frisk right up with her tail wagging to kiss him enthusiastically. She was also wont to contribute to the ambiance by going downstairs to pee on the landlord's rug. Our landlord was Judge Sam Houston Clinton, now on the court of Criminal Appeals: he tended to be a little humorless about those episodes.

Her politics weren't all bad: she once bit hell out of Col. Wilson Speir, head of the Texas Rangers. Shit never met another dog she didn't like and on the whole she liked people indiscriminately as well. She did have, however, strong prejudices against bicycle riders, uniformed law-enforcement personnel, and pregnant women. She spent much of her waking life getting into the neighbors' garbage and was fond of strewing it about generously. The acquisition of food was her major life interest and for this purpose she developed a fabulous impersonation of a starving dog. The fact that she was grossly fat much of her life only made the impersonation more impressive. Shit also liked to sleep a lot and never failed to sack out where she would cause maximum inconvenience, at the exact center of the traffic pattern, so people would either have to step over her or trip over her.

I never intended to name the dog Shit. Kaye Northcott foisted the little black puppy off on me with a heartless ploy —left her with me "just for the weekend" and then returned Monday threatening to take her to the pound and have her put to sleep. I was going to name her something lovely, like Athena, but reality intervened. She was the only dog I ever saw that could trip on the pattern in the linoleum, so we called her Shitface for a while, and then it got to be Shit for short and then it was too late.

In her younger years, Shit loved nothing so much as going on camping trips, where the opportunities for getting into trouble were almost limitless. Any trip on which she did not manage to fall into the cactus, steal the steaks, and turn over a few canoes, she considered a waste of time. I developed nerves of tungsten.

When I took Shit to New York in 1976, many people told me it was cruel to keep a ranch-raised dog in a big city. Of course she adored New York—so much garbage to get into, so many other dogs to meet, so little exercise. In a city full of Tsing Luck-poos and Shar-peis, people would look at Shit and say, "Oh, what breed is that one?"

"Purebred Texas blackhound," I always said, and they would nod knowingly and say they'd heard those Texas blackhounds were splendid dogs.

Shit once caused gridlock on the entire Upper West Side. I had found a parking space right in front of my building and so let Shit out of the car off her leash, as it was only a few steps to the door. Most unfortunately, a bicycle rider passed at that very moment. Shit charged into the street barking and snapping at the man, who had a baby in a small seat on the back of the bike. I tried not to call the dog in public, but I could see her knocking over the bike and the baby getting hurt. Clearly an emergency, so I let loose, "SHIT! SHIT!" This caused several neighborhood children to appear out of nowhere and to begin chanting in chorus while pointing at me, "She said a dirty word, she said a dirty word." The guy on the bike, justifiably upset about having been attacked by this beast, got off in the middle of the street and wheeled around yelling, "I'll have the law on you, lady. Letting your dog run loose without a leash is illegal in this city. That animal is a menace. I'm calling the cops."

In the meantime, a woman with an unrelated grievance over the parking space I had just occupied came marching down the block, arms akimbo, saying, "You have some nerve, you went right ahead and took that parking place, you saw us waiting there, but you went right ahead and took it, I can't believe your nerve, we were there first but you took that place. . . ." The kids kept chanting, the biker kept screaming, the lady kept bitching, Shit started running around everybody in circles, traffic came to a halt, then backed up through the red light, then two red lights, people got out of their cars to see what was going on, other people farther back started honking. Shit was delirious with the excitement of it all, the cops came, she attacked the cops, by this time traffic was backed up all the way up Amsterdam and down Columbus. A typical Shit performance.

I loved Shit, but she was quite wearing. I used to think wistfully that other dogs got dognapped or hit by cars. . . . Then one day, Shit did get hit by a car, but she didn't die: it just cost me $700 to get her leg fixed. She gimped around thereafter on this bionic leg, becoming more Shit-like by the year. The dog was a catalyst for trouble, disruption, uproar, consternation, confusion, and bedlam.

She went out with the style we had come to expect from her—hit by a car, but no mere dead dog by the side of the road. Nope, biggest mess you ever saw and it had to be cleared up by Northcott and myself. We got most of her remains into Kaye's plastic laundry basket and took her down to the pound, the two of us a pair of poorly matched pallbearers. The people at the pound were kind, but said they had to fill out a form. They needed my name. My address. And I waited one last time for the question I had answered a thousand times from bemused strangers, enraged neighbors, at kennels, veterinarians' offices, dog pounds, and police stations. "What is the dog's name?"

I had Shit for almost fifteen years. It seemed longer.

Louis Bromfield

DOGS OF MALABAR FARM
. . . AND BEFORE

The boxers began with Rex, a king among dogs. He arrived one afternoon at the house in France, big, golden brown with a muscular body, a black face on a snub bulldog head, a broad chest, an appearance of great ferocity and an air of great dignity. He was the gift of a friend and he had been spending several days with her twelve Norwegian elkhounds in her house near Chantilly. Now elkhounds are not exactly lap dogs and they can fight like demons and they resented the presence of the newcomer from Germany. There were three days of fighting and in the end, Rex the boxer won, if not the victory, the right to go his dignified way, unmolested. He arrived at our house with the sense of victory still strong in him.

It was not like having a puppy arrive in the house. That was an experience we had had countless times, mostly with Aberdeens, for we had come to have several dogs instead of merely one because when anything happened to one the sense of loss was too great. So we were always having new litters of puppies or buying new ones. Later we discovered that having more than one dog didn't make much difference because each one has its own personality and is an individual and when he dies, the sense of loss is not softened by the fact that he left behind several companions.

Rex was the first grown dog who had ever come into the house, and it would be hard to imagine a dog of more awe-inspiring appearance. I get on well with dogs but I confess that on first sight I had my doubts about getting on with Rex. He came into the room with an air of complete self-assurance. He did not wag his tail or growl or sniff about. He walked in with dignity and stood there looking at us. It was clear that we were not looking him over. The process was quite the reverse. He was a personality with great dignity who expected no nonsense and no familiarity. With some misgiving I patted his head and spoke to him. He neither growled nor wagged his tail. It was as if he were permitting graciously a favor.

That night I fed him and took him to sleep in my room. He went along graciously but with the same dignity and detachment, and in the morning when I wakened he was there on the rug beside me, awake, with his head between his paws, watching me out of his big brown eyes. It was then I think I realized for the first time what lay behind the eyes—the affection, the devotion, the loyalty, the dignity and the independence. But still he gave no outward sign, either of affection or even acceptance. When I went downstairs he went with me into the garden and while I had breakfast he sat in the dining room near me, never begging, taking no notice of the fact that I was eating. He had been a show-dog and like all boxers was a gentleman. I did not know then that he had never really had a master or lived with a family and that he was desperately hungry for a master to whom he could attach himself.

For three days he lived with us, still with the same dignity and detachment, never once growling or wagging his tail, and then on the fourth morning, when I wakened, he got up off the rug and came and put his big head on the bed beside me and looked at me with his great brown eyes. He did not wag his tail. He simply looked at me. I put out my hand and rubbed his ears and I knew that we were friends. When we went downstairs he went up and sniffed at each member of the family and did the same trick of resting his head on their knees and then suddenly he wagged his stump of a tail. He was telling us that he had accepted us after looking us over for three days. From that moment on there was never a more devoted dog. He took over the whole family. He watched the house. He was happy really only when the whole family was at home and together. Even then he kept trying to round us up and keep us all together on the terrace or in the library or the salon. We were his responsibility. When part of the family went to Paris for the day, he would sit all day listening for the sound of the car, an old Peugeot, which he could distinguish from every other car passing the house. When he sprang up and barked and ran to the garden gate, you knew the family had returned safely and he would be happy again, because we were all together under his watchful eye.

As the days went by his character softened and at times he would become almost demonstrative, although he never lost his dignity and he was always a little ashamed of displaying any emotion. I think he must have had an unhappy experience as a puppy, of being shipped about at dog shows and finally sold and put on a train and shipped to a foreign country and sent to a strange house filled with strange dogs where he had to fight to assert his domination. I think he had come to distrust all people and perhaps all dogs. That is why he had looked us over until at last he decided that we were all right and that he had no reason to distrust us. I do not use the word fear for there never was in Rex in all his life any sign of fear.

In the house at Senlis, he had two rivals, one of whom he dominated, the other he never managed to subdue although she weighed less than one of his own big paws. The first was the grandfather of the Aberdeens—a grizzled, tough old Scotty called Dash. Dash was both a tramp and a Don Juan. All the town knew him and certainly every lady dog in the town was acquainted with him. He would fight dogs of any size. I have seen him lying on his back snapping and biting at a sheep dog four or five times his size until the bigger dog would yield the day.

There was a square in the town where all the stray dogs had a habit of gathering, perhaps because in the square there were three butcher shops with open fronts and the butchers had a habit of throwing scraps into the street for

the dogs to fight over. When any of the family went up the
hill to the market, Dash always went along. He liked any
excuse for going to town. And when you turned into the
square Dash would rush forward at full speed into the
midst of the little army of mongrels sunning themselves or
scratching peacefully on the cobblestones. At sight of him
they would scatter in all directions into alleys and door-
ways. He never failed to perform this same trick.

He was, in addition to being a tramp and a Don Juan, a
good deal of a show-off. He knew all the butchers well and
his showing off paid good dividends, for the spectacle of the
fleeing dogs always amused them. When the square was
cleared, Dash, sometimes accompanied by a lady dog, would
quietly visit each shop in turn and receive scraps which he
devoured in peace without any vulgar fighting.

Every family in town with a bitch sooner or later would
announce that their bitch had had puppies and that Dash
was the father. They always had a certain pride in the
event since Dash was not a mongrel but a *chien de race,* a
pedigreed dog, and that, no matter what the breed or ances-
try of the female, made the puppies in French eyes, distinguished and valuable. But of all his conquests the most re-
markable was that of a huge German police dog bitch called
Marquise. She was the property of Picquet, the gardener,
and I doubt that a more ferocious dog ever lived. She had
come to Picquet full-grown and most of her life she had
spent chained to a laundry delivery wagon. She appeared to
hate all mankind and all other dogs. Picquet kept her attached to a kennel by a heavy chain near his house in the
vegetable garden and each time anyone opened the gate,
she would lunge forward growling and showing her teeth.
She grew steadily more savage until, fearing for children
and guests and even for myself, I asked Picquet to get rid of
her.

Picquet himself, was what might be called a "natural." He
was not very bright but he had a wonderful way with flowers, vegetables and animals. I doubt that anyone else living
could have gotten on with Marquise. He came from the Pas
de Calais and spoke the ugly half-Flemish Pas de Calais
patois. He could wait on table, take care of the pony and the

children, poach trout out of the clear-running Nonette by luring them with Swiss cheese or stunning them with *eau de Javelle*. Together he and I grew wonderful vegetables and flowers and I learned from him many a trick about gardening and farming which I hope never to forget. I think in all that world he was the only person who loved Marquise. I promised him another dog if he would send her away.

He agreed as to the danger of having Marquise about, but asked that he might keep her a little longer. She was, he said, *enceinte*, which in English merely meant that she was about to have puppies. I received this news with astonishment as I knew that not only was Marquise kept chained up but that the garden was surrounded by a high wall topped with broken glass which no dog, not even a St. Bernard, could cross. The only dog who ever came into the garden was Dash who worshiped Picquet and left him during the day only on the occasions when he went to market to break up the dog *Kaffeeklatsch* in the Place Gallieni and receive his daily handouts from the butchers. Considering the difference in size between Dash and the ferocious Marquise, a mating seemed highly unlikely. I said to Picquet, "But what dog could be the father? No dog but Dash ever comes into the vegetable garden."

Picquet bowed his head and said, *"Mais monsieur, J'ai aidé un peu"* (I gave a little help).

Marquise remained until she had weaned her puppies and then went off as the companion of a forester living in a lonely house on the road to Aumont. Everyone was happy, including Marquise, for in the forest she could run at liberty. Picquet kept two of the puppies who grew up into odd-looking dogs—half-pint police dogs with smooth black coats, Scotty heads and magnificent sweeping black tails arching over their backs.

On one occasion Dash very nearly destroyed a famous dog, the handsome white poodle called Basquette, belonging to Gertrude Stein. Basquette, a big pink and white dog, trimmed and tonsored always by the best dog hairdresser in Paris, arrived with Gertrude for lunch one Sunday and Dash, after one look at Basquette, decided, I think, that the poodle was not a dog at all but some monstrous, strange, unknown animal that asked for extermination, an intolerable sissy to a tramp Don Juan like Dash. In any case, he leapt to the attack and while the pampered, marcelled Basquette howled, Dash went for him. Two tables were overturned, one guest kicked accidentally in the shins by another and two others bitten before Basquette was rescued, his beautiful marcelled white coat streaked with blood.

Only once did Dash ever attack a human, and on that occasion I felt that he was justified. His victim was a pompous bore, the town jeweler, by name Monsieur Bigué. It has often been said that bores recognize and avoid each other but this was certainly not the case with Monsieur Bigué who had chosen to marry a bore even greater, if possible, than himself. By some ill fortune, the pair had one of the common gardens which adjoined our own and they had a dreadful habit of leaning over the fence to make long, involved, formal and deadly conversations on politics, the weather, the foreign exchange. They were childless and incredibly avaricious as only a French provincial jeweler can be. Madame Bigué lavished all her affection upon a wretched little female pocket-sized dog called Frou-Frou which fortunately never left the jewelry shop or house save to go into the little walled garden at the back. No virgin heiress was ever protected as fanatically as Frou-Frou. She was, I think, the only female dog in the town which Dash had not seduced. Madame Bigué would, I think, have preferred the grave to bringing Frou-Frou with her when she and her deadly husband came to work their little garden or sit in the summerhouse which dubiously ornamented it. Dash's evil reputation had long since preceded him.

For years Dash took no notice of Monsieur Bigué although he passed the kitchen steps almost daily, always carrying an umbrella and a basket. (In addition to being bores, they were a mistrustful, suspicious pair, who never for a moment trusted anyone or anything, even the weather.) Then one morning without visible provocation, Dash sprang from the kitchen steps and tore the seat out of Monsieur Bigué's pants as he passed with his basket and umbrella. Marguerite, the fat cook, rescued Monsieur Bigué and when I heard of the incident I went to wait upon Madame Bigué at the jewelry shop. She received me with dignity as I explained my regrets and said that I wished to make reparation.

All would be forgotten, said Madame Bigué (while the virgin Frou-Frou yapped in some hidden portion of the house) if Dash were left with the veterinary until it was determined whether he had hydrophobia and if I paid the doctor's bill and for a new suit of clothes for Monsieur Bigué. It just happened, said Madame Bigué, that Monsieur, although he was bound to work in the garden, was wearing his best suit, and as it was obviously impossible to buy a new pair of pants that would match the rare pattern of Monsieur Bigué's choice. A mere new pair of pants wouldn't suffice, it had to be a whole new suit. I inquired for Monsieur Bigué but was told that he was prostrated and that his leg was swollen to elephantine proportions.

The story ended happily enough. I paid the doctor's bill and bought a new suit for Monsieur Bigué. Dash, it turned out as I expected, did not have hydrophobia. I think he merely had great wisdom. I never knew whether Dash attacked the jeweler because he had heard about Frou-Frou and the seclusion in which she was kept or whether he did it because Monsieur Bigué was an intolerable bore and Dash could not support watching him pass one more time with his basket and umbrella. I only know that if Dash hadn't attacked him, I should have bitten Monsieur Bigué one day myself.

That then, is the history and character of Dash, not a dog who after ruling the dogs in his own house and indeed in all the town, would welcome the arrival of a big boxer from Germany.

On the first morning after Rex's arrival, the two dogs encountered one another in the garden. They did not growl. They did not sniff at each other. As for Rex, he walked past Dash with perfect dignity, ignoring him. For once in his life Dash did not attack on sight. His tail went straight into the air and twice he walked the length of the garden on his toes, very stiff-legged, every hair on end. He attempted to ignore the big bulldog but couldn't quite succeed. He kept watching him out of the corner of his eye, sizing him up. For once, it seemed, he decided he had met his master. Presently, with an air of the utmost casualness and dignity, he re-entered the house and went through it to his post on the kitchen steps where he could watch what went on in the street and attack any unfortunate dog who happened to pass by. As a tramp, the kitchen steps were just the place for him.

Relations between the two dogs never improved although they continued to live in the same house. When they encountered each other, Rex ignored Dash and Dash walked past Rex with the aggressive stiff-legged dignity of a very small Scot. Rex was the only dog that Dash failed to attack in the whole nine years of his life. I think it was not the size of Rex which awed him for he had fought even bigger dogs and sent them howling down the street; it was the awful, regal manner which Dash had never encountered among the mongrels of the town . . .

When life in Senlis came to an end forever and we left the old house by the Nonette, George took Rex with him on the "Normandie" straight to America since the quarantine on dogs in the British Isles made it impossible to take him with me to London.

Dash was dead, having passed away of premature senility, owing, I think, to a disreputable but highly enjoyable life. The one remaining Scotty, not a very bright or affectionate dog, I left with a friend. Sita too was gone, after having become paralyzed from having too large a litter of kittens by an alley tomcat. The old life had come to an end.

In London I heard only assurances, mostly from Tory friends, that there would be no war, that Mr. Chamberlain and the Conservative party had arranged all of that. "Peace in our time!" was a phrase which became more and more insipid and unreal and maddening to someone who had been living on the continent of Europe for the greater part of eighteen years and who had heard at dinner parties in London and Paris, Madrid and Rome the talk of the politicians who had brought about the débacle.

It was that awful period in London when the English seemed blind and deaf, when there were still people in the government like Lord Londonderry, who believed "the Germans were really a very nice people, so much like ourselves." The atmosphere became unendurable and at last one night when I found myself making an angry speech in the Savoy Grill, I decided it was time to clear out. I loved England. I had had many happy adventures there. My impulse was good. Like so many other good friends of England I wanted to warn them. It seemed to me that all but a few of the English—Vansittart, Eden, Duff-Cooper, Rebecca West Churchill and in general the "French faction"—were like spoiled, stupid children.

The next morning I called the United States Lines and managed to get a cabin aboard the "Manhattan," feeling in my heart that I would never again find the England I was leaving. I went alone to Paddington and just as the train was about to pull out I saw Mito Djordjadze, tall and dark and Georgian, running toward me. He was carrying a puppy, quite a big puppy, in his arms. As he came near I saw that the puppy was a boxer, not a golden one like Rex, but a dark brindle with a black face and one white paw.

Breathless, he said, "I've brought you a wife for Rex!" And I remembered the promise of Mito and his wife Audrey that they would one day give us a mate for Rex.

I took the puppy into my arms and realized that she was thin and ill. "It's the best I could find" said Mito. "You went off in such a hurry. She's just gotten over distemper. The kennel people say she'll be all right."

The train started and I jumped aboard with a puppy I hadn't expected.

There was trouble about keeping her in my compartment and I went to the luggage van and sat there all the way to Southampton. If ever a dog could not be left alone, it was that puppy. She was ugly and thin and ill but in her eyes there was something which I think I recognized even then as humor and gaiety and independence.

Aboard the ship she had to stay in the kennel on the top deck with the other dogs, but I spent nearly the whole of every day with her and saw to it that she got warm milk and brandy. Most of the time she lay listlessly in my lap, but she attracted an admirer who evidently liked frail ladies. He was the biggest, ugliest English bulldog I have ever seen. His name was Harry and he had a heart as big as he was ugly. He was being shipped to a kennel in America and he had no master but he soon took care of that by adopting me and the pup. All the way across the Atlantic he insisted on lying on the bench beside us with his head on my knee. By the time we reached New York I would have bought him if I had known whom he belonged to. We said good-by to Harry and he was put back in his box to be shipped someplace in New England. I have never seen him since but he was one of the most charming, if sloppy personalities I have ever met.

It seemed obvious that the wife of Rex should be called Regina and so that became the puppy's name. She was still very sick while I stayed in New York and most of the time she spent on a sofa in my mother's flat, languishing like a mid-Victorian invalid.

Like many a woman who is never strong until she has a baby, Regina was sickly until she had her first litter of six pups at Malabar. From that moment on she was strong as an ox. Since then she has had twenty more pups and is many times a grandmother, but even today none of her grandchildren are gayer or stronger. She has always been a good mother but a stern disciplinarian with no Oedipus nonsense about her. With each litter there comes a time when she feels they should go on their own and out they go. She will have no more of them but in an odd fashion she continues to discipline them. Even though Prince, her eldest son, is only about eighteen months younger than herself, she will take no nonsense from him or from any of her other children or grandchildren. She is affectionate but independent and hardy, and often enough when all the other boxers are inside in winter, Gina stays out sunning herself by the greenhouse with the cocker spaniels.

Rex and Regina became the founders of a long line of boxers at Malabar. Three of their sons—Prince and Baby and Smoky—still are there and will be till they die. Their brothers and sisters are scattered all over the country, with owners who feel about boxers as we do, that there is something special about a boxer which makes them different from other dogs. There is a kind of fraternity among people who own boxers. You can speak to them on the street although they are total strangers and stand there indefinitely talking about the virtues and personality of the breed. I have in my life owned fifty or sixty dogs of many breeds and I have always made friends with dogs, even with poor savage Marquise, but the boxer is different from them all. He is stubborn and gay and comical. He may be devoted to you but never in a worshipful way. He knows your faults and accepts them. He is not a pet. He is a companion and friend and equal. Wherever I go on Malabar, five or six boxers go with me. They are as companionable as any friend. They race off after rabbits, vainly, for they have little nose and none too good sight, but their sense of hearing is fantastically acute which accounts, I suppose, for the fact that they have always been watch and police dogs. Their origin as a breed is somewhat obscure. But there is one story that they are one of the oldest breeds in the world, coming originally from north China where they guarded caravans and compounds, and indeed it may be true for the ancient stone dogs one sees in China guarding the entrance to compounds are very like the modern boxer.

They are good farm dogs for they do not go off hunting as hunting dogs will do nor run across country chasing cattle or killing sheep like the terriers . . . They are happiest when they are with people and rarely go a hundred yards from the house unless someone goes with them. To them the prospect of going for a long walk across the fields is as exciting as going for a walk can be to a dog bred in a city apartment.

The children of Rex and Regina each has his own personality. Prince, the eldest son, never leaves me by more than three feet from the time I rise in the morning until I go to bed at night. There is nothing groveling or worshipful in his devotion. It is simply that I am his best friend. He understands now that when I go away, it's not for good and that I always come back, but the mere sight of "store" clothes brought out of the cupboard throws him into a depression. From that moment on until I leave the house, he sits at a distance from me watching every move with a sad reproachful eye. Even when I get into the car to go to the station, he will not come near me. He is a great worrier and always filled with anxiety.

His brother, Baby, was in a sense an orphan, for he was the only one to survive from a litter born prematurely to Regina after she threw herself gaily into the middle of a dogfight. He was brought up on a bottle by Venetia Wills, who as an evacuée from bombed England was staying with us, and he has his own special character. He is both a born farmer and a clown with a great attachment for the horses. All his days are spent out-of-doors on the farm, mostly with Charley Martin, who runs the vegetable garden and does a bit of everything. He will spend a whole day walking up and down a field beside the horses when they are plowing, perfectly happy. He has never been popular with the other dogs, chiefly I think, because they recognize him as a show-off and a ham actor. He drinks Coca-Cola from a bottle and water straight from the tap, lapping the water as it falls. To him a wheelbarrow was meant to ride in and if he is with you working in the garden, he will jump into the wheelbarrow the moment it is empty and stay there until he is wheeled up to the house. But his best trick is his high-diving from the high platform into the pond just below the Big House. With a running start he will go off the platform at a height of twelve feet and leap twenty feet into the water for a stick. Despite the fact that boxers are not water dogs and Rex and Prince had to be driven outside on a rainy day to step high and with distaste in the wet grass. Regina, Baby and Smoky take to the water like retrievers. I think this is so because they grew up with two cocker spaniels and a golden retriever who, even in zero weather, would break the ice of the pond, go for a swim and then come out and roll in the snow. During the hot days of midsummer, Regina will sit in the pond a whole morning with only her head above the water, looking for all the world like a rather ugly hippo.

No one on the farm ever bothered to teach them any tricks, for there was never time. Baby invented all his bag of tricks, begging as a born show-off to perform the high-diving stunt whenever visitors arrived. He is the only one of the dogs who holds long conversations with you, answering each question with different intonations, a trick which infuriates the others, notably his older brother, Prince, who, since the death of Rex, has taken over as boss of the farm dogs. He keeps them in order, aided by Regina who has never given up disciplining them, even Prince; and as Baby grew older, he turned out to be the only rebel against authority. The rebellion leads occasionally to fights such as took place more and more frequently as Rex grew old and ill and was no longer able to assert his authority. And a fight among four or five big boxers is a terrifying spectacle to behold for one not used to them and unable to assert his authority. I have scars on one wrist and one ankle where Prince, in the midst of a fight, got hold of me instead of Rex or Baby. His shame when he made the discovery that it was I he was biting, was moving to behold.

In the evenings all four, Regina, Prince, Baby, Smoky and a newcomer called Folly, come into the house and now and then stage a fight which wreaks havoc. As the source of most such rows is usually the question of who can sit or lie nearest to me, the fights are likely to take place under a card table. As a fight between two becomes a general brawl, cards, drinks, score pads and all are likely to go flying into the air. Now and then a fight occurs under a table with *bibelots* or a vase of flowers and the result is the same. On occasion the breakage has been expensive. The most celebrated fight of all took place under the dining room table during a children's party with twelve kids present. Before it was stopped, two chairs were broken and there was milk, cake and ice cream on floor, walls and ceiling.

Big dogs, indeed, have no place in the life of demon housekeepers. Fortunately, all our household prefers dogs to an immaculate house. The five boxers sleep in my room which serves as office, bedroom and workroom and fortunately is on the ground floor and has many windows and two outside doors leading into the garden. Prince sleeps on the foot of my bed, Folly in a dog bed at the foot, Gina on the sofa and Smoky and Baby on chairs. Although Baby has long outgrown the chair he chose as a puppy and hangs over both ends, nothing will induce him to give it up. Each place belongs to a different boxer and if one attempts to take over the property of another, the fight is on. Now and then, other members of the family complain that my room is a little "high" and Nanny attacks it with Lysol, taking over usually while I am away and cannot protest. I am afraid that I prefer the smell of dogs to the smell of Lysol.

Last summer a guest observed, "I can't believe this house is new. It looks so old and well-worn. Nothing looks new!" to which George replied, "Dogs and children take care of that. It looked like an old house six months after it was built."

Prince has his own intelligent tricks. The doors of the house do not have knobs but French door handles and almost at once Prince learned that he could open any door at will by turning the handle. It is impossible to shut them in any room. The moment a breakfast tray goes into the bedroom of any guest, it is a sign to the dogs that the day has begun and a procession led by Prince who opens the door, visits the guest. They learned long ago that few guests resist the impulse of feeding them bits of toast and bacon.

Prince not only opens all the doors inside the house but learned long ago to open not only the outside doors, which do not have handles but thumb catches, and to hold back the screen door while he opens the main one. He knows too how to open the doors of an automobile and more than once visitors have looked out of the window on cold days to observe five or six boxers sitting in their car with the doors all *closed.* For Prince learned too that closing the door behind him prevents cold air and drafts from entering the car.

But the ancient Ford station wagon is their delight, for they know that when any of us get into it, it means that we are off to some remote part of the farm where the other cars cannot go because of the mud or the roughness of the roads and fields. In summer in the early morning they will go and sit in it to prevent its getting away without them. Once it arrives in a big field they are all out at once to run and hunt. They are not clever hunters and the only thing they ever catch is ground hogs which abound over the whole of the thousand acres. They know every ground hog hole on the whole of the farm and long ago learned the trick of going straight to the lair as quickly as possible to get between the ground hog who may be out feeding and his safe, underground lair. Each one of the dogs, as a pup, had a good mauling by a big ground hog and the lesson has never been forgotten. Rex, the German, nearly lost an eye in his first encounter. A big, old ground hog can weigh as much as forty pounds and will fight and claw like a wildcat, but the boxers learned long ago that the trick is to get their opponent behind the head and break his neck. It is all over in a second.

Although killing anything gives me no pleasure, the dogs do serve as a check on the ground hogs which otherwise might dig us out of house and home, for with lynx and wildcat and wolf gone from our country there is no longer any natural check on the ground hog. No fox dares attack them. Their digging can start bad gullies and they can destroy a whole young orchard in a week or two. There are still plenty of them left to dig holes and make shelters not only for themselves but for rabbits and other game. A female raccoon, hard put to it for a lair in which to have her young, will share a ground hog hole with the owner.

There are plenty of dogs on the place for Bob has a female boxer called Kitchey and Kenneth one called Susie Parkington who also knows the Ford station wagon trick. If Susie sees or hears the station wagon she will come across country any distance to join in the picnic.

There is no more sociable dog than a boxer and there is nothing they like so much as visitors or a party. As they come rushing out they are likely to scare people to death, since they are ferocious in appearance, but they are in their hearts all amiability. In that respect they are ideal watchdogs on a place like Malabar where there are hundreds of visitors a year. No one can come near any building without the boxers knowing it and setting up an uproar, but biting is not a part of their natures. The golden retrievers were different for nothing could persuade them that a part of their duties as watchdogs was not to *bite* and on occasion they went beyond bluff and took pieces out of Charley Kimmel, the game warden, whom they knew well, and out of two or three other visitors. In the end we gave them away, although they are the most beautiful of dogs.

The boxers, used to square dances and picnics and meetings, learned long ago that a group of automobiles meant a party and a party meant that they were going to have a feast of hot dogs, of steak bones, of pie and cake and doughnuts. No party ever had more welcoming hosts than the boxers and the two cockers on the occasion of farm festivities. Usually the next day meant indigestion for them and the consumption of great quantities of grass and zinnia leaves, which boxers seem to regard as a cure for indigestion. But apparently the party is always worth the indigestion.

I cannot write of the dogs at Malabar without mentioning the two small female cockers, Patsy and Dusky, who came to the farm as pets of the children. Dusky is all black and very feminine and very sporting. When the dog party goes out in the old station wagon, Dusky and Patsy would go off hunting, *really* hunting and not just rushing about rather aimlessly like the boxers, deep into the woods to come back all wet or covered with burrs hours later. They were inseparable companions who lived out-of-doors and slept in the potting shed, silky, affectionate and charming.

Of the two Patsy had the eccentric character. She was a very small cocker, black with tan-colored spots and big brown eyes with a slight squint which gave her a hopelessly comic expression. Despite her small size and good nature she took no pushing around from the big boxers. Although in play they sometimes sent her rolling end on end, she always came back making hideous snarls and growls. In a way, her life was a tragedy of frustration for her one overwhelming desire was puppies. With her first litter she caught pneumonia and all of them died. Shortly after that she ran under a car and suffered a broken pelvis. It mended badly and after that there was danger in her having puppies and we did not breed her, but twice each year she had an hysterical pregnancy even to producing milk. Whenever Gina had puppies which was about once a year, Patsy acted as nursemaid. Apparently she and Gina had some agreement for although Gina would allow no other dog, male or female, to come near her puppies, she made no objection to Patsy sitting beside the straw-filled box in which they lay or even to sharing the box with her and her puppies. Patsy would never leave the vicinity of the box save to eat and when Gina went out she would get into the box with the puppies and even attempt to feed them. I think she got satisfaction out of all this and she helped Gina to bring up four litters of pups which before they were three months old were twice as tall as Patsy herself.

This last summer she showed all the signs of hysterical pregnancy again and none of us, accustomed to the phenomenon, took any notice. But this time the pregnancy was real. Somehow she had been bred, probably to one of the big boxers. The puppies were born dead and Patsy died too later, happy I think, in the illusion that again after years, she had produced a family. Anne wrote a poem about her—

It matters little to the world
That one small dog
No longer trots these dusty lanes.
The canny eyes, untidy hair
Brown dots for eyebrows
Have faded in the dark, unknown of death
Much like a pebble in a dark smooth pool.
Still she is here, trotting busily
The steep fern-covered hills
So long as we who were her friends, remain on earth.

Beth Brown

PREFACE

I once had a dog.

He was a Wire-haired Terrier with a family tree too tall to climb. And so I named him Hobo.

At the time it happened, I had a big town house on Riverside Drive. When you climbed the three flights of curving handsome white stairway, you stood in The Study—a huge, square room lined with books and a fireplace, its French doors leading to a garlanded balcony which hung over the majestic Hudson and invited the stars indoors.

It was here I wrote the many books which brought me fame and fortune. It was here I feasted from a bottomless golden cornucopia, filled to the brim with an exciting career, secretaries, servants, money in the bank, a diamond ring on my finger and an uncommon dog named Hobo.

Then death darkened my bright world. I lost both the man I loved and the dog who loved both of us. Death tapped me, too. I found myself high and dry, washed upon the lonely island of an empty life in an empty house with no desire to write another line.

There is no medicine like work. But my heart was hushed. My mind was a blank. The thirteen rooms in that prodigal house thundered with silence, as, day after day and night after night, I sat at my desk with apathy for ink in my inkwell.

The bank account dwindled. The servants departed. Rejection slips now filled the mail box in place of acceptances and checks. The world of Broadway where my name hung in lights as well as the publishing world which had first discovered me, now vanished like lost continents into outer space. My days of success were forgotten. My career as an author was over. I had drawn my will. There remained only the formality of drawing my last breath.

Then, one midnight, I heard familiar steps on the stairs.

I looked up as he came to the threshold and watched him cross the room—plumping down as usual at his usual place on my feet. He could have been a little ghost dog but his brown eyes were warm with life. His stubby tail thumped an audible Morse code on the wooden floor. He spoke as he always did—in a language we both understood.

"What are you doing?" he asked.

"Nothing," I answered back.

"Why aren't you writing?"

"What'll I write about?"

"No ideas?"

"No."

There was a moment of silence. That brown look eyed me intently. That small tail was loud in the room. Then he tossed me a challenge.

"Why don't you write about me?"

And with that, he was gone.

But the thought-form remained. The least I could do was catch it like a ball—and try tossing it back in the hope that somewhere—someone would catch it from me and begin to play ball again—learning as I had learned from one of the world's greatest teachers—my little dog—that joy is an inside job.

I sharpened my pencil. Somewhat fearfully, I went to work. I tossed off a dog story. My first. I took as my theme, the simple, unpretentious account of a little dog named Hobo—from the time he first climbed my stairs to my house —walked straight into my heart—and then down the five flights and into his blue inheritance.

I wrote the story as a short short, page or two, wide margins, double-spaced. I sent it out half-heartedly. It came back a dozen times or more. Finally, I sold it to an editor who did not want to buy my piece because King Features did not use any "pet stuff."

Then it was printed.

And then it happened.

The Miracle!

How could I count it for less?

The old house awoke one morning to a new life.

Thousands of people had read my story. Thousands of people wrote me thousands of letters. The post office wrote to me, too. It sent me a notice to please come in person and lug home the bulging sacks of mail.

By mail. By column. By radio. How other voices thundered praise. Kate Smith read the story and plugged it on her show. Walter Winchell lauded Hobo in his column. Several magazines bought rights and reprint rights. A publisher contracted for me to take the two small pages and make them into a book.

All Dogs Go to Heaven eventually made its bow, and became a best seller, propelled, I am sure, by the power and the love of a little dog who used the invisible bridge beyond to help me to my feet.

That one dog book broke the dam. Other dog books followed. The books turned into record albums such as *School Book For Dogs*. The book *Hotel For Dogs* became a successful radio show, which ran, coast-to-coast daily for three years on N.B.C. with Quaker Oats as sponsor.

The show gave birth to litters not only of numberless dog stories but to cat stories and even horse stories, to animal articles and animal anthologies—no end in sight—with one little dog named Hobo—at the head of the Pet Parade.

No doubt he enlisted St. Francis of Assisi to help me in my need. No doubt he corralled an invisible army of four-legged brothers and sisters. No doubt he did his best to ferret out the ghost dogs of the earthly famous and sent his messengers to scurry back in night-mares on the pillows of editors and publishers the name of Beth Brown and her work!

I don't know what he did—but he did it. Enough for me to say to you that I made a major discovery—as no doubt you have—that our dogs—in our times of need—return to serve us.

Ben Hur Lampman

WHERE TO BURY A DOG

A subscriber of the Ontario *Argus* has written to the editor of that fine weekly, propounding a certain question, which, so far as we know, remains unanswered. The question is this: "Where shall I bury my dog?" It is asked in advance of death. The *Oregonian* trusts the *Argus* will not be offended if this newspaper undertakes an answer, for surely such a question merits a reply, since the man who asked it, on the evidence of his letter, loves the dog. It distresses him to think of his favorite as dishonored in death, mere carrion in the winter rains. Within that sloping, canine skull, he must reflect when the dog is dead, were thoughts that dignified the dog and honored the master. The hand of the master and of the friend stroked often in affection this rough, pathetic husk that was a dog.

We would say to the Ontario man that there are various places in which a dog may be buried. We are thinking now of a setter, whose coat was flame in the sunshine, and who, so far as we are aware, never entertained a mean or an unworthy thought. This setter is buried beneath a cherry tree, under four feet of garden loam, and at its proper season the cherry strews petals on the green lawn of his grave. Beneath a cherry tree, or an apple, or any flowering shrub of the garden, is an excellent place to bury a good dog. Beneath such trees, such shrubs, he slept in the drowsy summer, or gnawed at a flavorous bone, or lifted head to challenge some strange intruder. These are good places, in life or in death. Yet it is a small matter, and it touches sentiment more than anything else. For if the dog be well remembered, if sometimes he leaps through your dreams actual as in life, eyes kindling, questing, asking, laughing, begging, it matters not at all where that dog sleeps at long and at last. On a hill where the wind is unrebuked, and the trees are roaring, or beside a stream he knew in puppyhood, or somewhere in the flatness of a pasture land, where most exhilarating cattle graze. It is all one to the dog, and all one to you, and nothing is gained, and nothing lost—if memory lives. But there is one best place to bury a dog. One place that is best of all.

If you bury him in this spot, the secret of which you must already have, he will come to you when you call—come to you over the grim, dim frontiers of death, and down the well-remembered path, and to your side again. And though you call a dozen living dogs to heel they should not growl at him, nor resent his coming, for he is yours and he belongs there. People may scoff at you, who see no lightest blade of grass bent by his footfall, who hear no whimper pitched too fine for mere audition, people who may never really have had a dog. Smile at them then, for you shall know something that is hidden from them, and which is well worth the knowing. The one best place to bury a good dog is in the heart of his master.

Ruth Pollack Coughlin

LUCY NEVER HAD A BONE TO PICK—SHE LOVED UNCONDITIONALLY

The first time ever I saw her face, she was six weeks old. Among her seven sisters and brothers, all of whom gained my attention, she was the only one who, when I picked her up, looked me square in the eye and then nestled her tiny head in the hollow of my neck.

I was sold, and she was for sale. It was 1978. It was December, and I had just turned 35. In New York in those days, I had grown tired of taking care of nothing more than a group of plants. Thriving as they were, those plants, they were not showing a lot of heart, and heart was what I needed.

Twenty-five dollars is what the animal shelter on Long Island told me it would take to liberate this creature, silky and black as India ink and a mixture of at least two breeds, with a minuscule diamond of white on her miraculously small breast. On the way home, in the car I had rented to drive across the bridge and bring us back to Gramercy Park, she curled her body next to mine and rested her face on my right thigh.

It is true that she sighed. It is true that I, a woman without children, attempted to understand that this puppy I had just named Lucy was not a child. It is also true that I could feel my own breast swell, my heart fluttering, my mind filled with the possibilities of unconditional love—mine for her, hers for me. Unconditional love: It was something I knew most people felt could only be doled out by a mother, even though many therapists acknowledge that family love, especially mother love, can be as polluted as the biggest and the baddest and the nearest toxic dump.

Lucy, in growing up, ate couches. She ate books and records and pillows and eyeglasses. She nibbled at fine Persian rugs. She ate shoes. She believed that the legs of very good chairs were her personal teething rings; she hid her rawhide bones in the pots of those well-tended-to plants, and then she would rediscover those bones quite dramatically, fresh dirt strewn across varnished hardwood floors. She scratched, and scratched again, at the surfaces of treasured antique chests.

Rolling against a tide of family and friends who castigated me for accepting such bad-dog behavior, I stood firm. She destroys *things,* I said. These things are nothing, that's what they are, they're things, they don't live and they don't breathe. She doesn't destroy people. She'll grow out of it, I said. People who destroy people don't ever grow out of it.

And, of course, she grew out of it.

Those who admonished me and never loved Lucy didn't know that for every new couch I bought, that for every pillow or pair of eyeglasses I replaced, I never looked back. They didn't know that Lucy was there during the times about which they knew not.

She was there when I cried, and licked the tears off my face; she was there when I rejoiced, and cavorted around, laughing with me.

She knew what was good and she knew what was bad. When louts were cruel to her, I comforted her; when they were cruel to me, her instinct was such that she curled tighter around me.

Even then, in those early years when the dog-expert books said I should scold her—and I did—she never stopped loving me, nor I her.

No matter what, she would finally smile at me, as only dogs can smile. And always, it would be a smile that went beyond acceptance. It was much more: It was pure. It was without contamination. It was something called love with no baggage, something most therapists would not be able to acknowledge.

Away from the textbooks and the jargon, I was Lucy's god, and she was mine, a statement that has its ironic elements, insofar as I have not yet been able to decide whether there is a god or not.

She and I, transported both in spirit and in body by the man of our dreams, moved from New York to Michigan when she was five.

He grew to love her, as I knew he would, though at first it was slow going. Here was a man who had trained dogs all his life, and then here was Lucy—untrained except in one thing, loving me. He was the one who finally got it, truly got it, because he knew about a kind of love that held no barriers. Because he knew that this bond between Lucy and me was like our marriage. Incontrovertible.

When Lucy got sick on my birthday last month, exactly 13 years after the day I first saw her, I was optimistic.

For more than a dozen years, she had never been ill. Requisite shots, yes. Sickness, no. Romping and yapping and wagging her tail in her own inimitable Lucy way, she was perceived by the mailman, by the Federal Express and the UPS crew as a puppy. She was a dog who slept in the sunshine with her front paws crossed; she was a dog who was at my heels wherever I went.

She was someone who finally showed me the meaning of unconditional love. She was a dog who would never die, I thought, a Lucy who would continue to support me, who would be there, a dog who would see me through the darkest of anyone's worst imagination of what the bleakest days would be like.

We went three times, Lucy and I did, during those two weeks in December, to the veterinarian, surely one of the kindest and most compassionate people I have ever known. She was hospitalized, her heart failing, her kidneys not functioning, an IV unit hooked into her beautifully turned right leg, an inelegant patch marking where her once lustrous black fur had been shaved to accommodate the needle.

The vet allowed me to visit, but not for long, and from a distance. It might upset her to see you, he said, and then he added, if she actually does notice you, it might be disruptive for her to watch you leave. Not wanting to add to the pain she was already in, I peered through a window. She was listless, apparently unaware of my presence.

Maybe she couldn't see me, but she could still smell me, the person with whom she had been sleeping for 13 years, the person who could never tell her enough how much her love was valued. And how I knew, shrinks notwithstanding, that no one could ever get a bead on this, and if they did, they'd probably think it was bonkers and maybe they'd even have to go back to school to figure it out.

This was Lucy who was just barely hanging on, but evidently proud to do even that. My husband and I knew: She was very sick, there would be no recovery. She doesn't, my husband said to me, want to leave you.

Lucy and I went back to the vet.

He allowed me some time alone with her, the vet did, after he told me there would be no turnaround. This was a statement made shortly after the one in which he told me that it had to be my decision. Most people, he said, out of a need that is especially self-serving, prolong the lives of their dying dogs.

I knew what I had to do. Her suffering could not go on, not for another day, not for another hour.

For some time, I held her. I thanked her for being such a great pal. I kissed her repeatedly, on the top of her head and on her eyes. On her adorable nose and on her incomparable feet. On every part of the small body I had kissed at least a million times during the past 13 years. On her setter-like tail, even though she wasn't a setter, a tail that never stopped wagging.

On her heart that was failing, a heart that had beat so well, so true, a heart that could have, in a split second, taught a legion of therapists what unconditional love is really all about.

The other day, I somehow found the guts to open the envelope with the veterinarian's return address. Euthanasia, the bill said. Fifty dollars.

It seemed to me a small price to pay to allow Lucy, the one who showed me at every turn that she was all heart, to go in peace.

Steve Rubenstein

A VERY GOOD DOG IS WHAT
SHE WAS

Annie was a good dog. This might surprise anyone who knew her, but newspapermen are not allowed to bend facts. The truth is that Annie was the best dog around. I loved her and that's true, too.

Annie died on Wednesday on an operating table in Corte Madera, and I suppose this is her obituary. If you don't want to read an obituary about a yellow Labrador retriever, you might wish to turn the page, because that's what this is.

In obituaries, you are supposed to mention how many years old the subject was when she died. Annie was 0. She had yet to reach her first birthday. She was 11 months and 3 days old when her gentle heart stopped beating. It's not a long time to live unless you lived life like my dog did, which was pleasurably if not particularly honorably.

Annie enjoyed her 0 years. She spent them on Ocean Beach, chasing tennis balls. She spent them in the lake behind Stern Grove, swimming for sticks. She spent them in a house in Miraloma Park, chewing sofa cushions.

Annie had her own way of doing things, and it was rarely the right way.

She knew how to heel well enough to know she didn't care for it. She could fetch the newspaper, only to drop it half-way up the steps. She learned to stop chewing phonograph records about the time she learned to start chewing compact discs.

In her 0 years, she attended three weddings. One of them was mine. She was the ring bearer, a duty she performed with her customary enthusiasm and absentmindedness. The moment the parcel was fastened to her collar, she took off down the beach in pursuit of a spaniel.

My dog was just getting the hang of things. She could catch a Frisbee, sometimes. She could roll over, if nudged. She was developing a taste for bananas. When you die at the age of 0, you leave a lot of bananas uneaten and many of them are in a bowl by the sink. She left many uneaten Milk Bones, too, one of which I just pulled out of my windbreaker pocket.

Annie liked ice cubes, especially the way they slid across the kitchen floor. We called them water bones. She especially liked kicking them under the stove and watching me crawl around and fish them out.

And she liked to travel. In her 0 years, she climbed to the top of Multnomah Falls in Oregon, swam in the Rogue River, romped through a snowstorm near Truckee and ate a barbecue beef sandwich in San Luis Obispo. She visited Los Angeles, too, because she was in the back of my car and had no choice. She forgave me, in exchange for a Milk Bone.

On her last day we visited the dog run in Mill Valley. It was a favorite place, located enticingly close to the sewage plant. We played fetch with a tennis ball and then it was time to drop her off for her ankle operation. I kissed her on the top of her head before the man led her away. I was always kissing her on the top of her soft, fuzzy head. People said I kissed my dog too much, but it's not really any of their business, being as the practice was conducted between consenting parties.

A few hours later, the call came from the surgeon. The anesthesia reaction that had stopped Annie's heart was a 10,000-to-1 occurrence. And the bone chip in her ankle, which necessitated the operation, was a 100-to-1 chance.

You can work it out for yourself. You multiply 10,000 by 100 and you find that Annie was one dog in a million. That's what she was, officially certified. She was a good dog, too, but that's not official. You only have my word on it.

Albert Payson Terhune

SOME SUNNYBANK DOGS

A schoolteacher, looking back over his experiences with more than a thousand pupils, would find himself dwelling with special interest in recollections of at least nine or ten of them; nine or ten personalities so outstanding, for one reason or another, that they will not let themselves be forgotten or grouped with the vast majority.

It is so with my memories of the long line of Sunnybank dogs.

Soon or late, every dog master's memory becomes a graveyard; peopled by wistful little furry ghosts that creep back unbidden, at times, to a semblance of their olden lives. To outsiders, the past deeds and misdeeds of these loved canine wraiths may hold no great interest.

With this somewhat windy apology, which really is no apology at all, let's go:

Lad stands out as foremost of the dogs of Sunnybank. I have written his life saga; stretching its exploits through no fewer than three "Lad" books. So I need not go in for a wearisome retelling of his biography. A few episodes and characteristics, and then we'll pass on to the next cage.

He was a big and incredibly powerful collie, with a massive coat of burnished mahogany-and-snow and with absurdly small forepaws (which he spent at least an hour a day in washing) and with deepset dark eyes that seemed to have a soul behind them. So much for the outer dog. For the inner: he had a heart that did not know the meaning of fear or of disloyalty or of meanness.

But it was his personality, apart from all these things, which made—and still makes—him so impossible to forget. As I have tried clumsily to bring out in my three books about him.

He was immeasurably more than a professionally loyal and heroic collie. He had the most elfin sense of fun and the most humanlike reasoning powers I have found in any dog.

Suppose we talk about those traits for a minute or two.

The Mistress and I went to pay a call of sympathy on a lachrymose old woman whose arm had been broken. The fracture had knit. The victim was almost as well as ever. But she reveled in giving dramatic recitals of her mishap to anyone and everyone who would listen.

We took Lad along with us when we dropped in on the invalid-emeritus. Before we had been there five minutes, we had every reason to wish we had left him at home.

Not that he failed to behave with entire outward decorum. But he took much uncalled-for part in the conversation. The woman launched forth on a detailed report of her accident. She sprinkled the lamentable recital thickly with moans and groans and belching sighs.

Lad was enormously pleased with the performance. So much so that he elected to turn the dolorous solo into a still more doleful duet. Every time our hostess gave forth one of the many successive sounds of grief, Lad copied it with startling realism and in precisely the same key. In perfect imitation, he moaned and whimpered and sighed and emitted ghastly groanings.

Throughout, he was lying demurely at the Mistress's feet. But his eyes were a-dance. The plumed tip of his tail twitched uncontrollably. Lad was having a beautiful time. The Mistress and I were not.

We sought to keep our faces straight, as the woman's narrative waxed in noisy intensity and as Lad's accompaniment swelled to a crescendo.

Groan for groan he gave her and moan for moan. Carried away by his own brilliant enactment, his ululations increased in volume until they all but drowned out the sufferer's performance. It was a horrible duel of emotional expression. And Lad won it. For the woman paused in her jeremiad, and stared down at the statuesquely couchant collie in tearful admiration.

"Oh, he's wonderful!" she exclaimed. "Just *wonderful!* He understands all the agonies I've been through! And it almost breaks his heart. I wish some people were half as sympathetic as this poor dumb beast."

Lad, who for five minutes had been anything but dumb, eyed her in happy expectation; waiting for her to strike the next imitable note of grief, and yearning for a chance to resume his own performance. But there was no opening. The lament had shifted to clamorous praise of the dog's unbelievable comprehension and sympathy. And in the hymn of praise there were no alluring groans to copy.

We got away as soon as we could. If ever a dog merited rebuke for disgraceful impudence, Lad was that dog. But neither the Mistress nor myself had the heart to scold him for it.

With uncanny wisdom the collie had realized from the outset that the old lady was in no pain, in no real distress, that she was just airing her past trouble in maudlin quest for sympathy and in an orgy of self-pity. And he had joined blithely in the scene; in a spirit of straight ridicule.

In cases of genuine human distress or pain or misfortune, Lad's sympathy was ever eager and heartsick. But he had a whole-souled disgust for any form of faking; a disgust he took pleasure in showing most unmistakably.

Sometimes his guying took a subtler form. As when a man came here to see me on business—a man Lad disliked and distrusted as much as did I. The day was hot. The visitor took off his new pongee coat and laid it on the edge of the veranda. Then he began to talk.

He had an unpleasant manner and he was saying unpleasant things. I was hard put to it to remember I was his host, and to behave civilly to him. I found the effort more and more difficult as the talk went on.

Lad was lying beside my chair. As always, he sensed my mood.

With a collie's odd psychic powers he knew I was increasingly angry and that I yearned to kick the visitor off my land. The dog looked worriedly up into my face. Then he eyed my caller, and the tip of one of his long white eyeteeth peeped from under the lip that had begun to curl ever so slightly.

I could see the tiger muscles go taut beneath Lad's coat. I laid my hand on his head and whispered sharply:

"Quiet, Lad. Let him *alone!"*

All his adult life the dog had known the meaning of both those commands and the stark necessity of obeying them. Yet the Master was pestered by this obnoxious stranger. And, with Lad, that was not on the free list. Glumly he lay down, his eyes fixed alertly on the guest.

Then, stealthily, he got to his feet. With catlike softness of foot he crossed to the veranda edge where was draped the visitor's imported white coat—a garment of much value, even if not of many colors. To my shame I admit I saw the collie's progress without checking it. I had used up my whole day's stock of hospitality.

Lad lifted the snowy and costly coat from its place. He carried it out onto the muddy gravel of the driveway as tenderly as though it were a sick puppy. The owner was too busy orating to notice the rape of the garment. And I had not the good breeding to call Lad back.

On the driveway, Lad sought out a spot where was a smear of surface mud and silt as wide as a dining-room table—the effluvia of that morning's heavy rain.

With the same exaggerated tenderness he laid the coat atop the area of mud. Then, in very evident relish, he proceeded to roll on it, back and forth, several times. After which he proceeded to rub one of his heavy shoulders into the muddily crumpled British imported pongee, and then the other shoulder. He ended the desecration by rolling once more upon it.

Now to an outsider this shoulder rubbing and rolling might have had no significance, apart from crass mischief. A dogman would have understood the unspeakable black insult implied. For only into carrion—liquescent and putrescent carrion—does a dog roll and rub his body in that fashion. It is the foulest affront he can offer.

It was when Lad had completed his task of defilement as I have told it and was pacing back in majestic dignity to his place beside my chair, that the visitor's eye chanced to rest —first inquisitively and then in swift horror—upon his treasured white coat; or at the befouled bunch of muddy cloth which had been that coat.

Again I should have reprimanded Lad right ferociously. Again I did not.

In October of 1912 the Mistress was stricken with a long and perilous attack of pneumonia. It was a time of horror which even yet I don't like to recall. Through the endless days and the interminable nights Lad crouched against the door of her sickroom. He would not eat. If he were put out of the house, he would smash a cellar window, and, two minutes later, he would be back at his post outside the shut door.

Day and night he lay there, shivering, moaning softly under his breath. Doctor and nurse, coming or going, would tread accidentally on his sensitive body a dozen times a day.

Outside, the October woods were full of chaseable rabbits and squirrels: Lad's lifelong pacemakers in wild-forest chases. But the dog paid no heed. Miserable and sick with dread, he lay there.

Then, of a glorious Sunday morning, the death danger was past. I called Lad into the sickroom. Trembling, ecstatic, he made his way to the side of the bed, moving as softly as any nurse or mother. The Mistress was told of his long vigil. And she patted his classic head and told him what a grand dog he was.

Then I told him to go outdoors. He obeyed.

Once outside, he proceeded to comport himself in a manner unworthy of a three-months puppy.

For the next ten hours complaints came pouring in on me: complaints ranging from tearful to blasphemous; complaints I was too happy to heed.

Lad had broken into the dairy, by hammering open its door with his head. There he had pulled, one by one, every milk or cream pan from the shelves, and had left the stone floor deep in a white covering.

Lad had chased the Mistress's cat up a tree. And the poor little feline was stranded out on the end of a wabbly bough whence only a long ladder could rescue her.

Lad had gushed forth among the cows and had driven them into stampede flight. One of them, tethered to a long chain, he had chased in a circle till the chasee was too exhausted to stand.

Lad had cantered up to the gate lodge. There he had slipped into the kitchen and had yanked from the open cover a ten-pound leg of mutton designed for the Sunday dinner of my superintendent and his family. This hotly savory trophy he had been burying deep in a flowerbed when the superintendent's wife rescued it in sorry plight.

Lad had nipped the heels of an elderly horse which drew a carry-all wherein his owner and the latter's children were driving to church. The horse had run away, more in conscientiousness than in terror, for several yards, before the driver could rein him in.

Meantime, Lad had sprung upward and had caught between his teeth the corner of an elaborate laprobe. He had dragged this for a quarter mile, and at last had deposited it in the dead center of a half-impenetrable berry patch.

Lad had hunted up three neighbors' dogs and had routed them out of their kennels and had bestowed on them a series of terrific thrashings.

Lad had ripped the nurse's best newly starched uniform from the clothesline (he hated the antiseptic-smelling and abhorredly efficient nurse from the first) and had deposited it in the black lakeside mud.

In brief, Lad had misbehaved as never before in all his stately life had he dreamed of misbehaving. He had been, for ten hours, a Scourge, a neighborhood Pest.

Fast and furious poured in the complaints from everywhere. To my lasting discredit, I must say I made the same reply to every weeping or cursing complainant:

"Let him alone. Send me the bill and I'll settle it. Lad and I have been through the red flames of hell, this past fortnight. Today he's doing the things *I'd* do if I had the nerve. We're celebrating, he and I."

(I don't need to point out to any of you that this was an inanely drunken speech for any grown man to keep on repeating as I repeated it on that golden Day of Deliverance.)

A year later, Lad took upon himself, of his own accord, a man's size job. Namely, the task of shaping his harum-scarum young son, Wolf, into a decent canine citizen. Patiently, the big dog wrought at this chore. At first the results were slow and uncertain.

For one thing, Wolf's inborn sense of mischief made his sedate sire's life a burden. The worst form of plaguing was the stealing by Wolf of Lad's most cherished meat bones.

At first the older collie suffered these thefts without resentment or punishment. Lad could thrash (and *did* thrash) every dog of his size, or much larger, which attacked him. But against a silly half-grown pup he would not employ his fearsome punitive powers. He hit on a better trick for keeping his beloved bones from Wolf's thieving teeth. I was lucky enough to be on hand, at a distance, to see this ruse carried out more than once. And, to me, it savors, not of blind atavistic canine instinct, but of true human sense of reasoning.

Lad received, as part of his dinner, a gorgeously meatful beef bone. He had eaten to repletion. Thus he planned to bury this delicious two-pound morsel for future exhuming and gnawing. First, he took preliminary steps.

Then with no show of caution at all he carried the red-streaked bone to a sheltered spot in a flower border. There he laid it down and proceeded to dig a hole in the soft loam —a hole deeper than he usually dug.

In the bottom of this pit he placed the bone. With his nose, he shoved an inch or so of earth atop the buried treasure. (A dog digs holes with his forepaws, you know. But he uses his nose, never his paws, for filling such holes. I don't know why.)

After the bone was comfortably if lightly covered, Lad dived into a clump of shrubbery hard by, and reappeared carrying a bare and sterile bone he had hidden there—a bone which long ago had lost its last iota of dog appeal and which had been bleached white by many rains.

This forlorn relic he dropped into the cavity. Then he proceeded to push back all the displaced dirt, up to the level of the rest of the ground; and walked unconcernedly away, not once turning to glance back at the cache.

Wolf had been watching from a safe distance, and with avid interest. As soon as Lad left the scene of interment, the puppy danced over to it and began to dig. Thus, often, he had rifled his sire's underground bone-repositories. Presently, Wolf had dug down to the first bone.

In disgust he sniffed at its meatless aridity. Then he turned away. Apparently he had had all his toil for nothing, for less than nothing, for a bone a starving coyote would have turned up its nose at. Off trotted the baffled puppy without the faintest suspicion that a right toothsome meat-fringed bone was lying less than two inches beneath the decoy bone he had disinterred.

Now, unless I am more in error than usual, that ruse of old Lad's called for something like human reasoning and powers of logic. Assuredly it was not based on mere instinct. Every move was thought out and executed in crafty sequence.

I have heard of two other dogs, since then, whose owners saw them do the same thing.

Let's go back to an aftermath of Lad's crazy spree of relief when he knew the Mistress was out of danger. A week or so later, the convalescent was carried downstairs, one Indian summer morning, and ensconced in a porch hammock. Lad, as always, lay on the veranda floor beside her.

During the forenoon, two or three neighbors came to see the Mistress, to congratulate her on her recovery and to bring her gifts of flowers and candy and fruit and the like. These presents they placed in her lap for inspection. Lad watched interestedly. Soon he got up and loped away toward the woods.

Somewhere far back in the forests he found—much more likely *re*found—the carcass of an excessively dead horse. From it he wrenched part of a rib. Then, dragging his heavy burden, he made his way home.

None of us noticed the collie's approach; the wind blowing from the wrong direction. Our first knowledge of his return to the porch was when he came alongside the hammock and dropped his awful gift across the Mistress' lap.

And why not? To a dog, such far-gone carrion is a rare delicacy. Not for food, but to roll in. To him the odor must seem delicious, if one may judge by his joy in transferring it to his own coat.

Lad had followed the example of the morning's visitors by bringing his dear deity a present—the choicest he could find.

After all, the reek of carrion cannot be much more offensive to us than is the smell of tobacco and of booze and of costly imported perfumes, to dogs. Yet for the incomprehensible pleasure of being near us, our dogs endure those rank smells; while we banish from the house any dog whose fur has even the faintest reek of carrion.

Of all my countless ignorances of dog nature, the densest is his yearning to be near his master or mistress.

I don't know why my collies will leave their dozing in front of the living-room hearth for the privilege of following me out into a torrent of winter rain. They hate rain.

I don't know why all folk's dogs risk gladly a scolding or a whipping by breaking out of a room or a kennel into which they have been shut, and galloping down the street or over the fields to catch up with the master who purposely has left them behind.

Today (for another and non-thrilling instance) I am writing at my hammock desk, a hundred yards or more from the house. Seven dogs are with me. It is a cool, brilliant afternoon; just the weather for a romp. The lawns and the woods and the lake all offer allurement to my collies.

What are the seven doing? Each and every one of them is lounging on the ground, close to the hammock.

Even crippled and ancient Sandy (Sunnybank Sandstorm) has left the veranda mat where he was so comfortable. To him all movement nowadays is a source of more or less keen discomfort. Yet he limped painfully down the six steps from the veranda to the driveway, and came slowly over to me, as soon as he found I was here; stretching himself at my feet, on bumpy ground much less comfortable than his porch bed. And here for the past two hours he has been drowsing with the others.

Why? *I* don't know. There must be some mysterious lure in the presence of their human gods which gives dogs that silly yearning to stay at their sides; rather than to do more amusing and interesting things.

When I chance to go from the house toward the stables, a cloud of the white doves of Sunnybank fly to meet me and to escort me in winnowing flight to my destination. There is no mystery about this semblance of devotion. They know their food box is in a shed there.

The same cause was assignable to the welcoming whinnies of my horses (when I still kept horses) that greeted me as I passed in through the stable doors in the early mornings.

It is the same with the goldfish, when a hundred of them converge in fiery streams to where I halt at the curb of the wide lily pool; and when they wriggle fearlessly in and out among my dabbling fingers. They know—or hope—I am there to feed them.

No, none of those phenomena holds a single half-grain of mystery, any more than does human fawning on a rich relative. But the dogs—mine and everyone's—stick around where we are and go where we go, through no graft motive at all.

They are absurd enough to want to be with us, and with no hope of reward. That is an impulse I have sought hard and vainly to explain to myself.

In the bunch of Sunnybank collies, as they lie around me here on the grass, there is no trace of the flattering attention they show toward the maids, who love to feed them surreptitiously from the kitchen windows; none of the still more rapt interest they bestow on my superintendent as he prepares their one ample daily meal.

There is no such patently self-seeking tinge in their attitude toward me as they lie here on the lawn. There was none of it in the canine procession which followed me to the house, three minutes ago, when I went to my study for a

new supply of typewriter paper, and which waited at the
door for me and then convoyed me back here to the hammock.

No, it is a trait I can't figure out. As I think I have said
several times in the past page or two.

Which is a long digression from our story. I like to hope it
hasn't bored you overmuch. And now let's get back to Lad:

I have dealt here only with a few of the queerly human
and mischievous and logic-guided happenings in Laddie's
life. Not with his actual history.

His death battle with two younger and stronger dogs in
the snow-choked forests back of Sunnybank, his deeds of
dashingly worshipful service to the Mistress and to myself
during his full sixteen years of life, the series of stark adventures that starred his long career—are not these chroni-
cled to perhaps tiresome length in my three books about
him?

Foremost among the Sunnybank dogs of my childhood and
young boyhood was my father's oversized pointer, Shot. He
is worth your notice. Naturally, in any modern dog show
Shot would be "gated" most unmercifully.

He was of royally pure blood. But his head lacked the so-
styled refinement of today's show pointer. His mighty chest
and shoulders and hindquarters that carried him tirelessly
for ten hours a day through the stiffest kinds of shooting
country, and the harsh coat and thick skin which served as
armor against briar and bramble and kept him unscathed
through the thorniest copses—these were at laughable variance with the silken skin and dainty narrow-chested body
lines of the show-type pointer of nowadays.

At "laughable" variance. But to me the laugh would not
be on Shot. For, to me, he still is, in memory, the grandest
pointer of my rather long experience.

My mother's health broke. My father took her and all of
us to Europe, in the hope of curing her. (The cure was made.
She lived more than forty healthy years longer.)

Sunnybank was rented during our two-year absence from
America. Shot was sent to one of my uncles to be cared for
until we should come back for him.

This uncle, Colonel G. P. Hawes, Sr., was an ideal sportsman. He understood dogs as it is given to few men to understand them. He and Shot had been good friends, since the pointer came to us as a just-weaned puppy. The dog could not have had a better home and a more congenial guardian.

Yet Colonel Hawes wrote my father that the usually gay dog had grown sullen and mopey and spiritless. Shot went through his duties in the hunting field as honestly as ever, but with no interest. He was grieving sorely for his absent master and for Sunnybank.

After our two-year exile we came back to America. One of my father's first moves was to go to my uncle's home and bring Shot to Sunnybank. He took me along on this errand. Its details are as clear in my memory as if they had occurred last month.

As soon as we were seated, Colonel Hawes sent a man to bring Shot into the house. The dog was kenneled some distance away and had not seen or scented our arrival. Into the living room plodded the pointer, at my uncle's summons.

He was thinner, much thinner, than I remembered him. His gait and his every line and motion were listless. He seemed wholly without spirit and devoid of any interest in life. My father had arranged the scene beforehand. He had told me what to do. I did it.

He and I sat motionless and without speaking. We were at the end of the room farthest from the door, and we were seated perhaps ten feet from each other.

Lifelessly, Shot came through the doorway. Just inside the threshold he halted. Up went his splendid head. His eyes sought out my father's mute and moveless figure. For a second or more the dog stood so.

Then he began to creep toward my father, hesitantly, one slow step at a time, crouching low and shuddering as with ague. Never did his dazed eyes leave my father's face. Inch by inch he continued that strangely crawling advance.

He did not so much as glance toward where I was sitting. His whole mind was focussed on the unmoving and unspeaking man in the chair ahead of him. So might a human move toward the ghost of a loved one; incredulous, hypnotized, awed. Then my father spoke the one word:

"*Shot!*"

The dog screamed; as though he had been run over. He hurled himself on his long-lost master, sobbing and shrieking, insane with joy. Then the sedate pointer whirled around him in galloping circles, and ended the performance by dropping to my father's feet; laying his head athwart his shoe and chattering and sobbing.

I drew a shaky breath. At the sound Shot raised his head from its place of adoration.

He dashed over to me and accorded me a welcome which ordinarily would have seemed tumultuous, but which was almost indifferent, compared to the greeting he had accorded my father. Then, all at once, he was back to his master again, laying his head on the man's knee and still sobbing in that queerly human fashion.

(Yet not long ago I read a solemn scientific preachment to the effect that no dog could remember a lost master's face and scent for the space of eighteen months! Shot beat that record by half a year. And I believe he could have beaten it by a decade.)

To Sunnybank we came; Shot with us. The dog's sullen apathy was gone—gone for all time. He was jubilantly happy at his return to the home of his earliest memories. But for weeks he would not willingly let my father out of his sight. He seemed to fear he would lose his master again.

My father taught me to shoot. A few years after our return to America he and I went out quail-hunting with Shot. At the base of a steep hill there was a brambly meadow. The meadow was cut midway by a railroad track. As he neared the track, the dog came to a dead point. He was facing a clump of low bushes on the far side of the rails.

Statue-still, Shot stood, at point, waiting my father's signal to move forward toward the clump. Before that signal could be spoken, an express train came whizzing around the curve at the foot of the hill, and bore down toward us. Under its wheels and in its wake was a fog of dust and of flying hot cinders.

Shot stood, rocklike, on his point. The train roared past,

not ten inches from his nose. The dog did not stir or falter, though he was peppered with burning cinders and choked by the whirlwind of dust and soot.

After the train had rattled its ill-smelling length out of the way, my father signaled Shot to move forward. The pointer took two stealthy steps ahead: steps that carried him to the center of the railroad track. From the clump just in front of him three quail whirred upward like a trio of fluffy little bombs. I suppose they had been too scared by the passage of the train to break cover until then.

Shot dropped to the ground, tense and waiting. My father brought down two of the birds in one of his customary brilliant left-and-right volleys.

I missed the third.

I was too shaky over the dog's peril and his plucky ignoring of it to do any creditable shooting just then. Shot lived to a ripe—an over-ripe—old age. We buried him in a strip of lakeside land a furlong or more from the house: a strip where sleep the Sunnybank dogs of almost eight decades. He was interred next to a grave whose little marble headstone's blurred lettering still may be deciphered as

> *FRANK Our Dog. For Thirteen Years*
> *Our Faithful Friend. Died 1876.*

Frank was Shot's immediate predecessor as my father's hunting companion.

Frank bit me when I was at the age of two. I had tried to bite off one of his floppy ears. It was a punitive nip Frank gave me rather than a real incision. I am told I wept loudly at the scare and hurt of it.

(If "when a man bites a dog, that's *news*," I wonder if it is tabloid news when a two-year-old boy chews a dog's ear.)

It was long before my birth that my father bought Frank. The dog was just past puppyhood. The time was winter. So my parents were at Newark, where my father was pastor of the old First Reformed Church. Not at Sunnybank. (Even as, to my sorrow, I was not born at Sunnybank like three of my nephews, but at Newark; because my birth date fell on December 21st—my mother's forty-second birthday.)

Young Frank was restless in his new home. On the day

after his arrival he ran away. My father and my mother and my two elder sisters and the servants went to look for him. All in different directions.

My mother wandered about for an hour, calling the pointer's name from time to time. At last, just in front of her, in the twilight, she saw him emerge from an alleyway. She called to him. He paid no heed, but walked away. She gave chase and overhauled him. The dog showed his teeth as she grabbed him by the collar. This though he had seemed to take a genuine liking to her after his arrival at our home.

She ripped a flounce or something from an underskirt—women wore a labyrinth of underskirts and petticoats in those prehistoric days—and fastened it to his collar. Then she proceeded to drag him homeward.

"Drag" is the right word. For the pointer fought and held back every step of the way. A small but enthusiastic crowd formed, and followed the pair with shouts of gay encouragement. After a mile of hard going they reached our house, at 476 High Street.

In triumph, if in much weariness, my mother hauled the snappingly protesting dog indoors and into the firelit living room.

There, in front of the hearth, lounged my father. Frank was asleep on the rug at his feet.

The runaway dog had tired of his roamings and, half an hour earlier, had come back home of his own accord; just as my father was returning from a fruitless search for him.

The dog my mother had kidnapped was enough like him to have been Frank's twin brother. They never knew who the other pointer belonged to. But when they let him escape into the night he bounded off as with some evident destination in view. For weeks thereafter my mother dreaded arrest on a charge of dog stealing.

Never again did Frank run away, throughout the thirteen happy years of his life. Every winter he stayed on at Sunnybank when the family returned to Newark. There, in the absence of his gods, he made himself a member of the superintendent's family at the gate lodge; waiting in weary impatience for the family's return home.

When in early spring our carriage and the baggage wagon turned in at the gate, Frank would follow them down the winding furlong driveway to Sunnybank House. Here, till our departure in late autumn, he remained. And he would bark harrowingly at the superintendent or at anyone of the gate-lodge household who might venture to come near our door.

He was a peerless field dog and a peerless watchdog. To the inch, he knew the boundaries of our land. No unauthorized outsider might pass those boundaries without instant challenge and assault from Frank. He treed several innocent (if any of their foul breed can merit the term, "innocent") sightseers. He was a Neighborhood Terror.

Nightly, at stated intervals, he would leave his porch mat and would patrol the outside of the house and every part of Sunnybank's home tract. He was perhaps the best of all the great Sunnybank watchdogs we have had over a period of nearly eighty years.

I never liked him. And he didn't like me. Thus, my praise of his worth comes from my brain and from my conscience, not from my heart. He was bitterly and justly resentful, too, when in his old age young Shot came here to take his place in the field work he no longer had the strength or endurance to perform. I can't blame the ancient dog for that.

It was soon after Frank's death that someone gave my mother a miniature black-and-tan terrier. She named her "Jip," after Dora Copperfield's tiny dog. Though Jip nominally was my mother's, yet the little terrier chose my father as her only god. Her devotion to him was all-engrossing. She insisted on going everywhere with him. Sometimes this was not wholly pleasant.

As when, one Sunday, she was locked safely at home in his study while the rest of us went to church. My father was in the midst of his sermon when Jip came strutting proudly up the aisle.

A servant had gone into the study to replenish its fire. Jip had sneaked out, unseen. Somehow she had made her way to the street. There she had had no trouble at all in picking up my father's trail and following it.

Happy at the reunion with her adored master, Jip eluded easily the grabbing hands of the sexton and of one or two of the worshipers whose pews she went past. Up the pulpit steps she bounded, and leaped to the pulpit itself, landing squarely if scramblingly on the open Bible.

My father did not so much as pause in the delivery of his sermon, nor did he heed the snickers of the congregation. Which showed fairly good self-control, I think, as he had not noticed the terrier's progress up the aisle, and as his first intimation of her presence was when she appeared, wagging her tail and wriggling with joy, on the top of the pulpit's Bible.

Without checking his discourse, my father picked up the little morsel of caninity very gently and thrust her into one of the flowing sleeves of his black clerical gown.

From that exalted position, her beady eyes surveyed the congregation in triumph. Throughout the rest of the long church service she did not stir. She just cuddled deep in the folds of her master's silken sleeve, her alert head alone visible to the grinning onlookers.

If she shamed us on that day, she more than atoned for her sin a few nights later.

Always she slept on the foot of my father's bed. He woke to hear her growling with falsetto intensity far down in her throat. Then she sprang to the floor and scampered out of the room and downstairs.

A moment later, the house re-echoed to her furious barking. My father went down to investigate. For never before had the good little dog done such a thing as to disturb the slumbers of the family. Others of the household also went downstairs to find what it was all about. As a result, a burglar was nabbed and jailed. In his cell, later, the man gave this testimony:

"The thing we're most scared of in a house is a small dog that barks and keeps backing away, like that black cur at Dominie Terhune's last night. You can't make them shut up and you can't get close enough to them to land a kick. They wake up everybody."

So much for gallant and adoring Jip. I don't remember what became of her. And now, a good deal more than a half-century later, there is nobody I can ask. Peace to her, any-how! She stood patiently for a godless lot of mauling from my grubby childish hands. I recall that much, very distinctly.

Jock and Jean were son and mother. Both were children of my great collie, Bruce, "The Dog without a Fault"; the hero of my book that bears his name.

Usually a mother dog loses all special interest in her pups soon after she has weaned them. That was what Jean did, in regard to most of her many offspring. But never with Jock.

To the day of Jock's death he was still her cherished baby. Daily—though he grew to be almost twice her size—she would make him lie down, first on one side and then on the other, while with her untiring pink tongue she washed him from nose to tail tip.

She superintended his eating. Daintily she would transfer from her own food dish to his the choicest tidbits of her dinner.

It was pretty: this love and care of the little brown collie mother for her big brown collie son. And Jock reciprocated it all to the utmost. He and Jean were wretchedly unhappy when either was forced to be away from the comradeship of the other for more than an hour at a time.

Jock was one of the best collies, from a show point, I have bred. Close he was to complete perfection. In his only dog show he cleaned up everything in his classes against strong competition; and he was beaten for "Best of Breed" only by his own peerless sire, Bruce.

This meant immeasurably less to me than did my success in breeding into him a clever and gay and courageous spirit and a flavor of wise "folksiness" which made him an ideal companion. Mentally, spiritually, in disposition, he was a replica of Bruce. I asked (and ask) better of no dog on earth. As to his jolly pluck:

From the time he could leave the brood nest, Jock feared nothing. He would tackle any peril, any adversary, with a queerly happy and defiant high-pitched bark whose duplicate I have yet to hear.

That queer bark of glad defiance was ever his war cry.

On a day, while I sat writing in my outdoor hammock, young Jock lounged at my feet. He leaped up, suddenly, with that jocund challenge bark of his.

I looked behind me. There I saw on the lawn a big and thick-girthed copperhead snake. The serpent had been gliding through the grass toward the hammock and toward my unheeding ankles, when Jock either had sighted him or else had become aware of the nauseous viperine odor—a stench as of stale cucumbers—which clings to such venomous snakes.

In some occult way, Jock had seemed to divine my possible peril. He had sprung up from his doze and had rushed at the copperhead, sounding his glad battle cry. The snake checked its own slithery advance. It coiled, and prepared itself to face this plangent new adversary.

Many a fool dog would have plunged forward to death. Many a more prudent dog would have avoided the issue. Jock was neither a fool nor prudent.

It was a new experience to me to watch his duel with the copperhead. Never before, I think, had he encountered a snake. Yet he fought with consummate skill. In and out he flashed, tempting the copperhead to strike, and then dodging back, barely an inch out of reach of the death-dealing fangs; and immediately flashing in with an effort to slay the serpent before it could coil afresh.

Each combatant was a shade too swift for the other. Back and forth for some seconds waged the death duel. Neither adversary scored the fatal bite, though more than once each was within a hair's breadth of it. And ever rang forth that odd battle bark of my young collie.

Then I had sense enough to realize that I was allowing an untried paragon to pit his skill, for life or for death, against the most deadly type of viper in this region. And I went to his help.

I smashed the copperhead's ugly triangular skull under my heel.

This with no zest at all. For I was wearing low shoes of canvas at the time. And if I had missed, the snake might well have scored on my unprotected ankle. I had a twinge of mental nausea as I gauged the distance and the required speed and accuracy for my head blow.

(There is little of the hero and a goodly modicum of the coward in my make-up. I detest danger and all its by-products. But Jock was my chum. And he was risking his life for me.)

The heel came down fatally on the fat copperhead. The fight was ended. So was the snake's life. And for two days thereafter Jock would have nothing whatever to do with me. I had spoiled his jolly life battle by butting in on it and by slaying his very entertaining opponent. He viewed me with cold aversion, until his youth and his inborn love for me overcame his disapproval.

But we were chums, he and I, for a pitifully short time after that.

For, a week later, like the fool I was, I took him to the dog show I have mentioned. He had been inoculated twice against distemper, and I used every other preventive and safeguard I knew of. (Doses of Delcreo in advance, a sponging of mouth and of pads with grain alcohol directly after the show, followed by the rubbing of flaked naphthaline into his luxuriant coat and a liberal dosage of castor oil.)

But a distemper-sickening chow had touched noses with him briefly at the big show. And that was enough. Jock was the more delicate because he was so closely inbred. He was infected. Ten days afterward he developed a dry cough and a wet nose.

The disease had set in. The malady which kills more pure-bred dogs than do all other diseases put together; the malady which took horrible toll from that same show and which has killed more than a thousand dogs a month, in its flood tide, after other shows.

Distemper practically never kills a mongrel (cross-breed is a better term) which it assails. The afflicted dog crawls under the barn or into some other cool and dark hiding place. Thence he emerges a few days later, bone thin and weak, but cured. But it slays at least fifty per cent of the thoroughbreds it attacks. Sometimes more.

It is a disease which, like typhoid, its human counterpart,

calls for twenty-four hours a day of nursing. And, as in typhoid, nursing is 90 per cent of the cure.

Not often does actual distemper kill its victims. Oftener they die of its sequel illnesses: pneumonia or pleurisy or chorea. Chorea is a form of St. Vitus's dance. With dogs, almost always it is fatal.

Jock weathered the distemper itself. I nursed him, twenty-four hours a day, through the pneumonia which followed upon it. Then through the long siege of chorea which came after pneumonia. I cured him of each successive one of these scourges, though I waxed dead on my feet from sleeplessness and from eternal vigilance during every one of them.

I gave up all attempt to work. And I spent my days and my eternally long nights in the wide box stall that was Jock's sickroom. Then, just as success seemed ahead, the youngster somehow acquired "re-infection." At least that is what the two vets named it.

At gray dawn of one November morning I sat on the floor in a dim corner of the box stall, with Jock's head and shoulders pillowed on my aching knees. I had had seven weeks of the conflict, with not one night's rest. Yet I was thrilled at the idea I gradually was winning the battle for the good collie comrade I loved.

Jock had been sleeping peacefully for hours. Suddenly he lurched to his feet. His fevered eyes were fixed on something in the black shadows at the far opposite corner of the wide stall; something my own gross human gaze could not see.

Forward he sprang, voicing that same strange high challenge bark of his. Then he fell dead, across my outstretched feet.

What did he see—if anything—lurking there in the stall's far corner? Probably nothing. Perhaps "the Arch Fear in visible shape." Whatever It was, brave young Jock had no dread of It. With his olden glad bark of defiance he had staggered forward to meet It.

Perhaps some of us soul-possessing humans may die a less valiant death.

At sunrise I had my men dig a grave for Jock, far from the

house, and in the center of the line of Sunnybank dogs' graves I have spoken of, at the lake edge and on the border of the more distant woods. There we buried the fearless young collie; buried him almost six feet deep, before we fumigated his box-stall sickroom.

For the past weeks Jean had been shut up in her own spacious kennel yard. That day I let her out, for the first time since her loved son had fallen ill. Eagerly, unwearingly, the little she-collie searched every inch of the forty-acre Place. Back and forth and in narrowing circles she coursed and cast, in quest of Jock.

After several hours she came to the grave of her puppy. There she halted; first sniffing about, then waving happily her plumed tail and nestling down beside the mound of new earth.

There was nothing sad or hopeless in her attitude and aspect. It was as if, after long search, she had arrived by chance at a spot nearer her precious son than she had been for weeks.

Presently she got up and ran to find me. Then she led me joyously to the grave; and once more she snuggled down to it, with waving tail and happy, smiling eyes. There she stayed all day. Not mournfully, but in pleasant expectation.

There was no taint of exhibitionism or of the role of professional mourner, or even of grief, in her bearing. She had missed her dear son all these weeks. Now at last she was nearer to him than she had been throughout that long time of waiting. Her sense of smell told her that.

Several times before settling down there she circled the ground, nose to earth, for a radius of perhaps thirty feet, as if in search of some newer trail to follow. There was none. She realized she was closer to him, at his grave, than anywhere else. Presumably she believed Jock would come back to her, there, in course of time. So she waited, in happy eagerness.

She did not establish a senseless twenty-four-hour-a-day vigil. But every morning, as soon as she was let out of her kennel yard, she would canter to Jock's grave in that same blithe expectation of finding he had returned. There she would stand or lie for a few minutes before going back to the day's usual routine.

She was a strangely lovable little collie, was Sunnybank Jean; with a hundred pretty ways that were all her own. The Mistress, whose property she was, used to say:

"Any burglar could steal Jean if only he'd pat her while he was doing it."

Unlike most of our collies, she loved petting, even from strangers. And she delighted in the arrival of guests.

At sight or sound of a car coming down the furlong of winding wooded driveway from the highroad above, Jean would run to the foot of the drive at the veranda's edge and stand wriggling with jolly anticipation, thrusting forward one of her white fore paws in an effort to shake hands with the approaching visitors—even while their car still was many yards away.

Two minor mishaps were forever befalling Jean. One was the wedging of some fragment of bone into the hinges of her jaw at the very back of her mouth. This propped her jaws wide apart and she could not close them or get rid of the obstacle. The other was throwing her shoulder out of joint during a gallop or a romp.

Both these things happened again and again. But they did not bother her. Invariably she would come straight to me with a flatteringly trustful expression on her visage; an aspect which said as plainly as could any shouted words:

"Boss, I'm in a jam again. But it's all right, now that you're here. *You'll* fix it for me. You always do."

With plumed tail awag, she would stand patiently and even gaily while I pried loose the lump of knuckle-bone from between her jaw hinges, or pulled the dislocated shoulder joint back into place.

One morning, when she was let out for a run, she went as always to Jock's grave. On her way back to the house she heard a car starting down the drive from the highroad. In her role of Reception Committee, she raced to her usual place of welcome and stood with fore paw outthrust in a handshaking gesture.

The car, laden with sightseeing strangers from far away, had crashed the gates at the lodge and had sped down the drive at perhaps forty miles an hour. This with the customary sweet disregard for the several "Please Drive Slowly" signs which disfigure our trees along the way.

Perhaps the driver did not notice the beautiful little collie near the veranda; the canine Reception Committee with waving tail and politely extended fore paw, waiting so happily to welcome the newcomers.

The car went over Jean, disemboweling her and breaking most of her bones.

She must have been in hideous agony during the few minutes before she died. But not so much as a whimper escaped her. She was as plucky as they make them.

When I ran out of the house, toward her, Jean lifted her head and turned it toward me with the same flatteringly trustful expression that always had been hers when her jaw hinge was blocked by a bone or when her shoulder was out of joint; the expression that said:

"It's all right, now that *you're* here. *You'll* fix it for me."

A large woman in bright blue was among the tourists who debarked tumultuously from the killer car. Breezing over to where I knelt beside my dead little collie friend she made graceful amends for everything by assuring me with a gay smile:

"I am really VERY sorry this has happened."

(What a heaven-sent gift it must be, to know how to say just the right thing at just the right time! Hers was a talent to be envied. Yet for the only time in my life I replied to a woman's words with a torrent of indescribably foul blasphemy.)

A local magistrate fined the head of the party one hundred dollars for trespass and for malicious mischief or for some such fault. He wanted to make the sum much larger. I persuaded him not to. I told him the mischief had not been malicious, but idiotic. Which was far worse, but not so heinous in the eyes of the law. Also that if he should fine every unwarranted sightseer motorist who trespasses on Sunnybank's posted grounds the national debt could be wiped out in no time at all.

I told him to divide the hundred dollars between two village charities. Which he did. I wanted no part of the blood money that he imposed for my collie chum's killing.

As far as I was concerned I thought the rotten incident was closed. It was not.

A syndicated newspaper column's space, two days later, was devoted to the affair and to denouncing me venomously for my boorishness in penalizing a party of "kindly meaning hero worshippers who had traveled so far to see me." Several papers throughout the country—one of them a religious weekly—printed editorials along the same general line of invective.

Thus I lost not only good little Jean, but much popular approval and, doubtless, many readers.

Daniel Pinkwater

THE SOUL OF A DOG

Once, Jill had fun with our Alaskan malamute, Arnold, by pretending that she was teaching him a nursery song. It was pure nonsense—Jill was tending our old-fashioned, nonautomatic clothes washer, and Arnold was keeping her company.

Jill sang him the song about the eensy beensy spider, and indicated where he was supposed to join in. He did so, with something between a scream of anguish and the call of a moose in rut.

The next time she had laundry to do, Arnold appeared, and sat squirming excitedly until she sang him the song. He came in on cue. Arnold learned a number of songs. His vocal range was limited, but his ear was good.

It was also Arnold who taught Juno, our other dog, to set up a howl whenever we passed a McDonald's. On a vacation trip, we'd breakfasted on Egg McMuffins for a week, and the dogs always got an English muffin. They never forgot.

I once observed Arnold taking care of an eight-week-old kitten. The kitten was in a cage. Arnold wanted to go and sleep in his private corner, but every time the kitten cried, he'd drag himself to his feet, slouch over to the cage and lie down with his nose between the wires, so the kitten could sink its tiny claws into it. When the kitten became quiet, Arnold would head for his corner and flop, exhausted. Immediately the kitten would cry, and Arnold would haul himself back to the cage. I counted this performance repeated over forty times.

Arnold acquired friends. People would visit him.

My friend Don Yee would borrow Arnold sometimes, and they'd drive to the White Castle and eat hamburgers.

He was the sort of dog you could talk things over with.

But he was not just a good listener, affable eccentric and bon vivant. He was a magnificent athlete. While Juno was tireless and efficient on the trail, Arnold made locomotion an art—a ballet.

Watching Arnold run flat-out in a large open space was unforgettable, and opened a window to something exceedingly ancient and precious—a link to the first time men followed dogs, and hunted to live.

He was a splendid companion—and he would pull you up a steep hill, if you were tired.

In a way, the hardest thing about living with dogs in modern times is related to the excellent care we give them.

Vast sums are spent by pet food companies devising beautifully balanced, cheap, palatable diets. Vet care these days is superb—and most pet owners take advantage of it.

As a result, dogs live longer than they may have done, and survive illnesses that they would not have survived in earlier times. And it very often falls to us to decide when a dog's life has to end—when suffering has come to outweigh satisfaction.

When it came Arnold's time to die, it was I who decided it. I called the vet and told him I was bringing Arnold in.

He knew about malamute vigor. He prepared a syringe with twice the dose it would take to put a dog Arnold's size to sleep. "Put to sleep" is an apt euphemism. It's simply an overdose of a sleeping drug. The dog feels nothing.

"There's enough in here for a gorilla," the vet wisecracked weakly. He was uncomfortable with what he had to do.

Arnold, of course, was completely comfortable—doing his best to put everyone else at ease.

I held Arnold while the vet tied off a vein.

"This will take six, maybe eight seconds at most," the vet said. He injected the fluid.

Nothing happened. Arnold, who had been completely relaxed, was now somewhat intent—but not unconscious, not dead.

"Sometimes it takes a little longer," the vet said. It had been a full half minute Arnold was looking around.

The vet was perspiring—getting panicky. I knew what he was thinking. Some ghastly error. The wrong stuff in the syringe. More than a minute had passed.

A crazy thought occurred to me. Was it possible? Was Arnold waiting for me to give him leave to go? I rubbed his shoulders and spoke to him. "It's OK, Arnold, I release you." Instantly he died.

I swear I felt his spirit leave his body.

The vet and I went outside and cried for a quarter of an hour.

He was an awfully good dog.

EPITAPHS . . . AND SUCH

Sir William Watson

EPITAPH

His friends he loved. His direst earthly foes—
Cats—I believe he did but feign to hate.
My hand will miss the insinuated nose,
Mine eyes the tail that wagg'd contempt at fate.

Lord Byron

EPITAPH TO A DOG

Near this spot
Are deposited the Remains
Of one
Who Possessed Beauty
Without Vanity,
Strength without Insolence,
Courage without Ferocity,
And all the Virtues of Man
Without his Vices.

This Praise, which would be unmeaning flattery
If inscribed over Human Ashes,
Is but a just tribute to the Memory of
"Boatswain," a Dog
Who was born at Newfoundland,
May, 1803,
And died at Newstead Abbey
Nov. 18, 1808.

When some proud son of man returns to earth,
Unknown to glory, but upheld by birth,
The sculptor's art exhausts the pomp of woe,
And storied urns record who rests below.
When all is done, upon the tomb is seen,
Not what he was, but what he should have been.
But the poor dog, in life the firmest friend,
The first to welcome, foremost to defend,
Whose honest heart is still his master's own,
Who labors, fights, lives, breathes for him alone,
Unhonored falls, unnoticed all his worth,
Denied in heaven the soul he held on earth—
While man, vain insect! hopes to be forgiven,
And claims himself a sole exclusive heaven.

Oh man! thou feeble tenant of an hour,
Debased by slavery, or corrupt by power—
Who knows thee well must quit thee with disgust,
Degraded mass of animated dust!
Thy love is lust, thy friendship all a cheat,
Thy smiles hypocrisy, thy words deceit!
By nature vile, ennobled but by name,
Each kindred brute might bid thee blush for shame.
Ye, who perchance behold this simple urn,
Pass on—it honors none you wish to mourn.
To mark a friend's remains these stones arise;
I never knew but one—and here he lies.

George Crabbe

QUATRAIN

With eye upraised, his master's look to scan,
   The joy, the solace, and the aid of man;
The rich man's guardian, and the poor man's friend,
   The only creature faithful to the end.

Elizabeth Barrett Browning

TO FLUSH, MY DOG

Loving friend, the gift of one
Who her own true faith has run
    Through thy lower nature,
Be my benediction said
With my hand upon thy head,
    Gentle fellow-creature!

Like a lady's ringlets brown,
Flow thy silken ears adown
    Either side demurely
Of thy silver-suited breast
Shining out from all the rest
    Of thy body purely.

Darkly brown thy body is,
Till the sunshine striking this
    Alchemise its dullness,
When the sleek curls manifold
Flash all over into gold
    With a burnished fulness.

Underneath my stroking hand
Startled eyes of hazel bland
    Kindling, growing larger,
Up thou leapest with a spring,
Full of prank and curveting,
    Leaping like a charger.

Leap! thy broad tail waves a light,
Leap! thy slender feet are bright,
    Canopied in fringes;
Leap! those tasselled ears of thine

Flicker strangely, fair and fine
      Down their golden inches.

Yet, my pretty, sportive friend,
Little is't to such an end
      That I praise thy rareness;
Other dogs may be thy peers
Haply in these drooping ears
      And this glossy fairness.

But of *thee* it shall be said
This dog watched beside a bed
      Day and night unweary,
Watched within a curtained room
Where no sunbeam brake the gloom
      Round the sick and dreary.

Roses, gathered for a vase,
In that chamber died apace,
      Beam and breeze resigning;
This dog only, waited on,
Knowing that when light is gone
      Love remains for shining.

Other dogs in thymy dew
Tracked the hares and followed through
      Sunny moor or meadow;
This dog only, crept and crept
Next a languid cheek and slept,
      Sharing in the shadow.

Other dogs of loyal cheer
Bounded at the whistle clear,
      Up the woodside hieing;
This dog only, watched in reach
Of a faintly uttered speech
      Or a louder sighing.

And if one or two quick tears
Dropped upon his glossy ears

Or a sigh came double,
Up he sprang in eager haste,
Fawning, fondling, breathing fast,
In a tender trouble.

And this dog was satisfied
If a pale thin hand would glide
Down his dewlaps sloping,—
Which he pushed his nose within,
After,—platforming his chin
On the palm left open.

This dog, if a friendly voice
Call him now to blither choice
Than such chamber-keeping,
"Come out!" praying from the door,—
Presseth backward as before,
Up against me leaping.

Therefore to this dog will I,
Tenderly not scornfully,
Render praise and favour:
With my hand upon his head,
Is my benediction said
Therefore and for ever.

And because he loves me so,
Better than his kind will do
Often man or woman,
Give I back more love again
Than dogs often take of men,
Leaning from my Human.

Blessings on thee, dog of mine,
Pretty collars make thee fine,
Sugared milk make fat thee!
Pleasures wag on in thy tail,
Hands of gentle motion fail
Nevermore, to pat thee!

Downy pillow take thy head,
Silken coverlid bestead,
          Sunshine help thy sleeping!
No fly's buzzing wake thee up,
No man break thy purple cup
          Set for drinking deep in.

Whiskered cats arointed flee,
Sturdy stoppers keep from thee
          Cologne distillations;
Nuts lie in thy path for stones,
And thy feast-day macaroons
          Turn to daily rations!

Mock I thee, in wishing weal?—
Tears are in my eyes to feel
          Thou art made so straitly,
Blessing needs must straiten too,—
Little canst thou joy or do,
          Thou who lovest *greatly*.

Yet be blessed to the height
Of all good and all delight
          Pervious to thy nature;
Only *loved* beyond that line,
With a love that answers thine,
          Loving fellow-creature!

William Cowper

EPITAPH ON FOP

Though once a puppy, and though Fop by name,
Here moulders one whose bones some honour claim.
No sycophant, although of spaniel race,
And though no hound, a martyr to the chase—
Ye squirrels, rabbits, leverets, rejoice,
Your haunts no longer echo to his voice;
This record of his fate exulting view,
He died worn out with vain pursuit of you.
"Yes—" the indignant shade of Fop replies—
"And worn with vain pursuit Man also dies."

AN EPITAPH, 1792

Here lies one who never drew
Blood himself, yet many slew;
Gave the gun its aim, and figure
Made in field, yet ne'er pulled trigger;
Arméd have gladly made
Him their guide, and him obeyed;
At his signified desire,
Would advance, present, and fire—
Stout he was, and large of limb,
Scores have fled in spite of him.
And to all this fame he rose

Only following his nose.
Neptune was he called; not he
Who controls the boist'rous sea,
But of happier command,
Neptune of the furrowed land;
And, your wonder vain to shorten,
Pointer to Sir John Throckmorton.

Robert Herrick

UPON MY SPANIEL, TRACIE

Now thou art dead, no eye shall ever see
For shape and service spaniel like to thee.
This shall my love do, give thy sad death one
Tear, that deserves of me a million.

William Wordsworth

TWO POEMS

I. INCIDENT CHARACTERISTIC OF A FAVOURITE DOG

On his morning rounds the Master
Goes to learn how all things fare;
Searches pasture after pasture,
Sheep and cattle eyes with care;
And, for silence or for talk,
He hath comrades in his walk;
Four dogs, each pair of different breed,
Distinguished two for scent, and two for speed.

See a hare before him started!
—Off they fly in earnest chase;
Every dog is eager-hearted,
All the four are in the race:
And the hare whom they pursue,
Knows from instinct what to do;
Her hope is near; no turn she makes;
But, like an arrow, to the river takes.

Deep the river was, and crusted
Thinly by a one night's frost;
But the nimble Hare hath trusted
To the ice, and safely crost;
She hath crost, and without heed
All are following at full speed,
When, lo! the ice, so thinly spread,
Breaks—and the greyhound, DART, is overhead!

Better fate have PRINCE and SWALLOW—
See them cleaving to the sport!
MUSIC has no heart to follow,
Little MUSIC, she stops short.

She hath neither wish nor heart,
Hers is now another part:
A loving creature she, and brave!
And fondly strives her struggling friend to save.

From the brink her paws she stretches,
Very hands as you would say!
And afflicting moans she fetches,
As he breaks the ice away.
For herself she hath no fears,—
Him alone she sees and hears,—
Makes efforts with complainings; nor gives o'er
Until her fellow sinks to reappear no more.

II. TRIBUTE TO THE MEMORY OF THE SAME DOG

Lie here, without a record of thy worth,
Beneath a covering of the common earth!
It is not from unwillingness to praise,
Or want to love, that here no Stone we raise;
More thou deserv'st; but *this* man gives to man,
Brother to brother, *this* is all we can.
Yet they to whom thy virtues made thee dear
Shall find thee through all changes of the year:
This Oak points out thy grave; the silent tree
Will gladly stand a monument of thee.

We grieved for thee, and wished thy end were past
And willingly have laid thee here at last:
For thou hadst lived till every thing that cheers
In thee had yielded to the weight of the years;
Extreme old age had wasted thee away,
And left thee but a glimmering of the day;
Thy ears were deaf, and feeble were thy knees,—
I saw thee stagger in the summer breeze,
Too weak to stand against its sportive breath,
And ready for the gentlest stroke of death.
It came, and we were glad; yet tears were shed;

Both man and woman wept when thou wert dead;
Not only for a thousand thoughts that were,

Old household thoughts, in which thou hadst thy share;
But for some precious boons vouchsafed to thee,
Found scarcely anywhere in like degree!
For love, that comes wherever life and sense
Are given by God, in thee was most intense;
A chain of heart, a feeling of the mind,
A tender sympathy, which did thee bind
Not only to us Men, but to thy Kind:
Yea, for thy fellow-brutes in thee we saw
A soul of love, love's intellectual law:—
Hence, if we wept, it was not done in shame;
Our tears from passion and from reason came,
And, therefore, shalt thou be an honoured name!

Thomas Blacklock

EPITAPH ON A FAVORITE
LAP DOG

I never barked when out of season;
I never bit without a reason;
I ne'er insulted weaker brother;
Nor wrong'd by force nor fraud another;
Though brutes are plac'd a rank below,
Happy for man could he say so!

Paul Schubert

MASCOT OF THE TEXAS

I first heard of him on July 3, 1919, the day I reported for duty aboard the battleship U.S.S. *Texas* in the Brooklyn Navy Yard. Nobody gave a damn about me, a newly appointed ensign joining his first ship. The officers of the *Texas* were preoccupied with weighty cares: Jim, I heard, was "under hack"—confined to the ship.

I thought Jim must be at least a lieutenant commander because of his evident importance. Later I discovered the officers were talking about a dog, the mascot of the senior officers' wardroom and a legend in the fleet.

Jim was under hack because of a recent misadventure. Like any other sailor, he liked to go ashore, and the last time the *Texas* had visited the Brooklyn Navy Yard he had walked down the dry-dock gangway and disappeared, AWOL. The *Texas* sent out search parties, notified the police, inserted newspaper ads—all to no avail. When the ship left the Yard bound for Guantanamo, Cuba, Jim was still missing. But when the rest of the fleet arrived there a signal message came from the *Utah:* "Send boat for your dog."

It seems that Jim had turned up at the fleet boat landing on the Hudson River, where the *Texas* normally anchored. He was dirty, exhausted, scarred from dogfights, and under his eyes were dark circles of dissipation. Fortunately a lieutenant on the *Utah* recognized him and took him aboard. At the time I thought the fuss exaggerated, but later I understood it.

Jim barely noticed me at first. He wasn't a snob; he was simply aware of his rank. I was a mere junior officer, and Jim didn't pay much attention to anybody in the J.O. mess. He had senior officers not only for intimate friends but for worshipers and slaves.

A year and a half later, when I became a Watch-and-Division officer and moved up to the wardroom, Jim was the first to congratulate me. From then on we were fast friends.

I lost my heart to that dog as I have never done to any other animal. He was a golden buff pit bull with wonderful eyes, the greatest intelligence, the most mobile and expressive face and the most communicative stub of a tail I have ever seen on a dog. Jim could express the gamut of emotions by a wiggle, a quiver or a wave of that stump tail. He could use it to question, invite, suggest, protest, implore.

Jim got his exercise chasing pennies. Invariably he had a copper cent in his mouth which he would lay at your feet, and when you kicked it he'd race after it. He would do this as long as your leg held out, then pick up his penny and go find somebody else. He had pennies stashed all over the wardroom and usually slept with one in his mouth. At mealtimes, though, the penny disappeared, and he got under the table and went from lap to lap, pushing his nose and eyes up under the tablecloth to tell you he was starving to death.

It bored Jim to do tricks. "Sit, lie down, roll over, dead dog, give me your paw," were too undignified for a first-class intellect. Jim's level was one of conscious thought. Whenever a wardroom officer started to put on civilian clothes, Jim would appear within two minutes and lay his collar on the deck (we never knew where he kept that collar, but he could always produce it) and ask to go along. He loved to go ashore and run and smell the smells and chase the ladies and have a hell of a time the way sailors do.

Jim was a good sailor in other ways. He didn't mind heavy weather. I can see him still, standing on the forecastle looking out into the gale with a critical eye, or sniffing the shore as the ship came into port and the breeze brought smells of land and harbor. And I swear he cast an eye aloft to see that everything was shipshape before we came to anchor. But he hated gunfire. The concussion of the salvos of ten 14-inch guns was torture to his ears. When shipfitters came below to put away breakables before the ship went to sea for a shoot, Jim would disappear into hiding. Days later, when it was all over, he'd come out looking dismal and gaunt.

For months Jim slept in George Breed's room. When George was detached from the *Texas,* I invited Jim to sleep in mine. There was no way of telling if he would accept; he was his own master when it came to choosing friends or quarters. I'll never forget my pleasure at seeing him push through the green door-curtain and come into my cramped little stateroom. I was at my desk, writing. He stood beside my chair for a moment, let my fingers stray over his head, scratch his ears and squeeze the small of his back. Then he circled on my rug, sank down, sighing contentedly, and made himself at home. He slept on that rug for the next two years. He liked a smelly old blanket spread all over him at night, and he'd snuggle around under it until it was suffo-catingly wrapped about him.

My room was 300 feet from the crew's galley and one deck down. But whenever the galley began cooking ham hocks he'd detect the odor through all the other shipboard smells of paint, tar, bright-work polish and below-decks stuffiness. In the middle of a night's sleep, with his head under the blanket, he would wake up and go to investigate. After a handout at the galley and a turn around topside he would come back.

Then he faced the problem of getting back under that blanket. No matter how warm the night, he would lie there and shiver so violently that finally I would wake up and pull the blanket over him. Then we'd both go back to sleep.

Jim was a great actor; he loved to show off, to have his collar shined up and take his place on the quarterdeck to help the guard, band and skipper greet the admiral as he came aboard for inspection. The part he didn't like was get-ting ready for inspection, which involved a bath. At the very word "bath" he would start to shiver, rolling his eyes and affecting a look of utter anguish. Gripping him firmly by the scruff of his neck, I'd take him into the shower with me and scrub him thoroughly while he licked the end of his nose to keep soap out of his nostrils. After I had dried him, he would prance off to show everybody how beautiful he was.

Nearly 40 years have gone by since I met Jim, but his personality stands out as vividly as that of any human I have ever met. He had the shape of a dog and therefore people thought of him as a dog, with the limitations of his kind. But Jim had no ordinary limitations: you didn't have to speak to him to make yourself understood. If you were miserable or sick, he was compassion itself. If you were happy, he was gay as air. If you gave him love, he gave back admiration.

There was one officer who didn't like Jim, and to that officer he gave back contempt. Jim entered his room only once, and then only part way.

That was one of the last times I saw him. In 1923, after a four-year cruise on the *Texas,* four of us got orders detaching us to other ships, and one of the four was the officer Jim didn't like. One evening about ten of us were sitting in this officer's room. We who were about to leave the ship felt a heavy heart. As we sat there talking, the door-curtain moved and Jim's head poked into the room. His mournful eyes passed from one to another of us, inquiringly. Then they fixed on the officer he didn't like, and I swear I saw a sardonic twinkle come into them. Jim opened his mouth, vomited copiously, then disappeared. That was his farewell to one he didn't care for.

He and I said good-by to each other casually, as shipmates do. As I left, he was standing on deck, watching the boat that took me away from the ship. I never saw him again.

The *Texas,* now permanently moored near Houston, is the only ship of her day that was kept as a monument of that naval era, thanks to contributions from the school children of the Lone Star state. The last time I went aboard, three or four years ago, a portrait of Jim still hung in the wardroom. I hope for his sake that there are plenty of pennies in heaven.

Raymond Carver

YOUR DOG DIES

it gets run over by a van.
you find it at the side of the road
and bury it.
you feel bad about it.
you feel bad personally,
but you feel bad for your daughter
because it was her pet,
and she loved it so.
she used to croon to it
and let it sleep in her bed.
you write a poem about it.
you call it a poem for your daughter,
about the dog getting run over by a van
and how you looked after it,
took it out into the woods
and buried it deep, deep,
and that poem turns out so good
you're almost glad the little dog
was run over, or else you'd never
have written that good poem.
then you sit down to write
a poem about writing a poem
about the death of that dog,
but while you're writing you

hear a woman scream
your name, your first name,
both syllables,
and your heart stops.
after a minute, you continue writing.
she screams again.
you wonder how long this can go on.

Bud Johns

REQUIEM FOR A
FIGHTING SPIRIT

Scoop and I took our last ride together today.

We've taken lots of rides together. He seemed to like being in a moving car, whether he was curled up under my legs, careful not to get in the way of the clutch, brake and accelerator, sitting on the seat next to me or, when he was younger, lying on the ledge behind the back seat. Before he went blind he took obvious delight in looking out the window at the passing scene.

I sometimes thought we should have written *Travels With Charley,* but Steinbeck and his standard poodle beat us to it. Besides, Scoop was a miniature and our travels together, especially the cross-country drives, always seemed to have a destination and scheduled arrival time instead of just rolling along taking things and places as they came.

That's the way it was today, too. My wife Judith's eyes were moist as she watched me lift the little gray bundle— one of our acquaintances referred to Scoop as "a Brillo pad" but what did he know?—into the car. She knew the time had come for the last ride—before the old dog's infirmities could become a source of irrevocable irritation to us and embarrassment to him—but that didn't make it any easier.

There was a destination today. We drove north across the Golden Gate Bridge, the same route we'd taken many times during the two years back in the early sixties that I'd lived in Mill Valley just after moving to the Bay Area. We were on our way to see Jim Steere, a good friend and veterinarian, and Scoop and I had certainly driven to the vet's many times in our seventeen years together.

There must have been some routine trips, for shots or something, but they're hard to remember. No wonder when you think of the other trips. Like the time he was little more than a puppy and the judge's Doberman lunged at him in obedience school and took a chunk out of the little fellow's side. That vet didn't think Scoop would live but he did, although he always had a thing about big dogs after that: I think he felt he'd been embarrassed in front of his master and he made it a matter of principle to attack any dog that was larger than he was. He could have saved me lots of anxious moments, plus quite a few bites and scratches, if he'd taken my word that I didn't doubt his courage.

Then there was the time he found and ate strychnine-laced meat left by some dog-hating sicko. He surprised the vet that time, too, but not before the reactions included the loss of nearly three inches off his tongue. He had to learn to drink all over, and never again was able to delight youngsters by lapping water from a Dixie cup on the floor.

Kids always liked him, although I remember one little girl who certainly wondered what a wonderful dog was doing with a miserable lying master like me. She was convinced that any little dog that could jump from the ground and bounce off the chest of a man six foot four had to be a circus dog; and she was scornful of me for not admitting it.

Actually we called him "a newspaper dog" and that's how he got his name. My then wife had never had a dog and decided she wanted one, but it had to be a poodle like the only dog she'd ever been around. I'd had lots of dogs as a kid and liked the idea, but one of those fancy little high-bred things wasn't my kind of animal. Still, I agreed to go look at the pups that were advertised, just so everyone realized we weren't going to buy one.

There were two, temporarily named "Boy" and "Girl" by the breeders, a young couple desperate to sell at least one before their puppy shots were needed. Their papers were impeccable—grandfather Ch. Barclay's Summer Smoke had been best of breed or best of show, I forget which after so many years, at Westminster—but the mother had died at whelping and the owners needed cash.

Of course, it was I who fell in love with "Boy," and there was a puppy in the car when we drove home. Mother and daughter were so surprised and pleased at my capitulation about owning a miniature poodle they insisted that I name it. Well, I was a newspaperman and his coloring was that of inky newsprint, he was just about the size of a flour scoop and scoop was a good newspaper word. He looked gray to me but I was told the poodle color was silver and, even though they're really a German breed, poodles are always French poodles, so what's French for silver? And the American Kennel Society accepted Ann's Scoop D'Argent as the registered name. Then, as if to confirm the validity of his name, his preferred location when I was working at home was lying on the inevitable pile of newspapers in the room where I was typing.

But we were talking about driving to the vet. There was the scary time he'd had a convulsion and the doctor said it was either something I've long forgotten the name of or, less likely, epilepsy. He gave us medicine for the former and said to come back if it didn't work. It didn't and Scoop and I drove back the next day, me with a record of observations and times from more than twenty convulsions Scoop had had the night before. The vet was amazed at the record, claiming he'd given special study to canine epilepsy in school but had never observed a seizure and knew of no observation record so detailed. Oh well, I was a newspaperman trained to observe and report and Scoop was a newspaper dog and the medicine the doctor prescribed the second time worked, but it did have to be given daily.

The dog's need for that daily medicine was responsible for much of what happened after that. He certainly wasn't responsible for the divorce, but my wife did insist on his custody, I'm sure because she knew I'd want him. That revenge quickly paled alongside the responsibility of making arrangements if there was to be an overnight absence or a weekend trip, and soon I got a call to take the dog or make arrangements to dispose of him. I found, and I guess it's not surprising, that there aren't a lot of people who want an old dog, (funny in retrospect, since he was only nine) who needs a pill every morning.

My traveling a lot and living alone in an apartment not suited for a dog was a problem, but not insurmountable when you figure Scoop had been paying his dues under frequently adverse circumstances and deserved to live under hopefully better ones. Fortunately there was the kennel in Pacifica that had seemed to be a good spot when he had been there on occasion and an arrangement was worked out for him to stay there except when I could pick him up for a weekend.

He was living at "his club" when Judith came into my life. She had a cat and, although he wasn't as old as Scoop, Yule's kitten days were far enough behind him that he wasn't immediately interested in accepting a dog into his life. It took him a while to realize that Scoop, already rapidly losing his sight because of cataracts, didn't represent a threat, and soon after the wedding the apartment on the top two floors of a four-story Victorian was a two-pet household.

The location of that apartment led to another emergency trip to the vet. Our landlady didn't like the idea of a dog in her garden so we kept the stairway down from the deck blocked with a folding baby gate.

One night I returned home from work and found neither Judith nor Scoop in the apartment. My first thought was that he'd had a relapse of a mysterious ailment and she'd taken him back to the vet. But when she returned I found that wasn't the case and we began our search. Down in the garden, dark by now, we heard a pathetic whimper and saw Scoop drag himself out from under the stairs.

It was easy to reconstruct what had happened. Scoop, who'd just had a haircut, remembered that pleasant garden and managed to squeeze through the gate but, being blind, had missed the steps and tumbled down two flights.

We watched anxiously as the vet made his examination and diagnosed a broken neck and right foreleg. Surely this was the end for the thirteen-year-old dog, but the vet, who'd taken care of him before, looked into Judith's tearful eyes and said, "I know this dog. He's tough. I think he'll make it." And he did.

Scoop's long life wasn't just a series of trips to the vet.

He even did some modeling. At least his tendency in later years to spend most of his time curled up resting on a cushion or rug made him an ideal subject for pen-and-ink drawings by Judith. And years ago, when I first moved to San Francisco, he was the subject of a much published photo.

A couple of years ago a friend, whom I consider the best photojournalist living, was completing a cover story photo portfolio on pets for a major national magazine. He'd actually completed it but was still hoping to add one more photo —"a great dog picture"—before publication. What did he mean by a great dog picture? He said he'd know if he got it but it would have the same kind of feeling as the one he considered the best dog picture he'd ever seen. Which was?

"Oh, you probably never saw it, but it was a little poodle standing on its hind legs, looking out through a knothole in a fence."

"I've seen it. I took it. That was Scoop, back in 1961." And Eddie, who thought of me with a typewriter instead of a camera and who had never known the crippled old blind dog as a frisky puppy, looked at both of us in a new light.

The photo was taken in the backyard of a flat on Greenwich Street where I lived my first three months in San Francisco. For some reason there were steps up from the yard to a board fence without a gate. But there was a knothole looking out on Blackstone Alley to the back of a Lombard Street motel and Scoop spent hours looking through that knothole at the activity outside the fence. I took the photo in question—and one from the other side—the day before I moved. A Sunday magazine bought and published both, then a major newspaper syndicate bought rights and distributed them, and the photo was even used on a "Hurry Back" greeting card.

These and other memories tumbled over each other on the last ride together. Joining them was the memory of another day four decades before when my father had to take Dixie, a much loved black cocker spaniel, to the vet after she'd been hit by a car. Later that day he asked me if I'd like to go with him when he made his calls and I did. I still remember his stopping at a country store, buying a Mounds and each of us having one of the chocolate-covered coconut sections. For years I remembered how he'd helped a little boy through that sad day but now I know I'd helped him, too.

The last ride together is over now and the grave overlooking the beach where Scoop used to run has been filled. He'd been a proud and trusting companion and I think he knew, as I do, how lucky I'd been.

Kenneth Rexroth

THE MOST NOTORIOUS FIGHTER IN ELKHART

I had a dog, a large brindle bull named Rex. He was an adult dog when we got him. He had been passed from hand to hand because he was a notorious fighter. Four other people had owned him, and a brother Elk or Mason gave him to my father. His name was already Rex before he entered the Rexroth family, where all dogs are named Rex whether male or female. We acquired him when we first moved into the Beardsley Avenue home while I was still a baby. He immediately became a devoted guardian, took care of me, and played with me all the time, but he remained the most notorious fighter in Elkhart. It was amusing to watch the other dogs in the neighborhood come down Beardsley Avenue. Rex would shift his weight and growl and they would cross the street rather than pass in front of our house.

After having been pulled and beaten out of fights and having had pepper thrown in his eyes and having been in all sorts of uproars in Main Street with all the dogs of all the leading citizens, he got into a fight with another bull which belonged to the man who had bought my grandfather's coal and lumberyard. This man came along with a stake truck, pulled one of the stakes out of the truck, and drove it down between the fighting dogs. He smashed Rex's skull and killed him and hopelessly crippled his own dog so that he, too, had to be killed.

Rex had been a friend of all the family and a companion to my grandfather and to Old Billy. Old Billy saw the whole thing from horseback and took after the man, who left his truck and fled to the lumberyard and ran upstairs to his office. Old Billy called up my grandfather, who was at the grocery store, and he came over to the lumberyard. The office building was one of those little two-story things peculiar to lumberyards with an office downstairs and a watchman's bed, I presume, upstairs. The murderer of the dog locked himself into the upstairs compartment. Billy was downstairs at the telephone holding guard, and the horses were coming into the gate of the lumberyard with the abandoned lumber truck when my grandfather came tearing over on horseback. This all sounds very Wild West, but normally nobody in my family rode horseback very much although we had saddles for everyone and all my grandfather's horses could be ridden. He came over with a Civil War musket, drunk. My grandfather stormed around downstairs, finally fired all his ammunition through the floor into the upstairs room. The other dog dragged himself home, badly torn by Rex, with his shoulder bone and front leg broken by his master, and had to be chloroformed.

The friendship between the two men had been close, and a great strain was put on it by all this dog killing and shooting. Nevertheless the death of the other dog, particularly since he had been killed by his own master, so upset everybody that the friendship was made up, mourning over the two dead dogs.

That's the only dog I had in my childhood. I have a memory of other brief periods when dogs were brought home or I found a dog that maybe stayed a week. We never had a regular pet after Rex and nothing ever took his place.

Thomas M. Boyd

FRED, A DOG GONE BUT NOT FORGOTTEN

It's tough to lose your shadow. Mine weighed 60 pounds, with a rounded nose and pointed ears that look like they had been inherited from Rin-Tin-Tin rather than Lassie. Though the patrician name of a purebred collie was scratched on a piece of paper somewhere, he responded simply to Fred. He was the dog I always wanted, and he was my friend.

For 10 years, from the time I picked him out of a litter of six until I carried him into the vet's office for the last time, Fred and I were virtually inseparable. In fact, we were apart only once, and that was while I was on my honeymoon. Even then, though out of sight, he was never entirely out of mind. In fact, I thought I heard thunder rumble the day I turned to my bride and said wistfully, "You know, I really miss ol' Fred."

During his life, which I think was a good one even by canine standards, Fred saw his role change from that of a nonpaying roommate to the surrogate child of newlyweds to the elder statesman of a growing family of five—counting Fred. Brooke, my seven-year-old daughter, first met him when he poked his moist, collie nose into her bassinet and introduced himself with an impromptu lick. My 16-month-old son received the same initiation when he joined the family.

Brooke learned to walk partly because of Fred—or Fef, or Fud, or Ferd, depending on her stage of vocal aptitude at the time. He became the prop against which she leaned when she tried to stand, and he stoically held his ground when she mercilessly tugged on his black and white coat in her first attempts to walk. He even taught her respect for traffic; whenever I instructed him to sit at intersections, she would watch him carefully and squat.

With Tyler's arrival in 1983, Fred's enthusiasm for the unpredictable moves of an infant ebbed. He had learned with Brooke to be wary of the crazed look of a 2½-foot kamikaze incapable of altering its course before impact. With Tyler, whenever Fred's ears detected the staccato sounds of rapidly approaching footsteps, Fred's eyes flashed open and his lumbering body headed for the door. In his last months, his hips didn't cooperate as they should have, and I couldn't avoid the sense that time had begun to interrupt Fred's longstanding role as tutor. His days with us were coming to an end.

What I always knew, of course, was that my furry friend's interest in my children was an excuse to stay close to me when the demands of others often seemed to interfere. For 10 years we walked the sidewalks of Alexandria, Va., together, three times a day, every day, and after the kids came he seemed to look forward with relish to those few undisturbed moments. He was always the first one awake when I got up in the morning, and as the day wore on, he would station himself against the front door until I came home. At 11 p.m., when his internal alarm dictated one last tour of the block, I could count on him to remind me. After all the lights went out, the last sound I heard was a sudden thump in the night, accompanied by a satisfied groan. Fred was asleep at the foot of the bed.

No matter when we took our walks, whether in the misty chill of a brisk, fall morning, or in the solemn quiet of a dark Virginia night, there was an unspoken kinship between us. And even as Fred's prance in time faded into a slippery shuffle, his eyes were always bright and direct, ever the good listener. The night before he left me, when his pace had slackened to that of the old man he had become, I sat down on some brick steps and gave him a hard, sustained hug. The full weight of his body leaned into me, and his long cold nose once again pried my palm from my leg and nudged it softly into the familiar position next to his right ear. I knew then he was saying "goodbye."

In the weeks since, I have found myself thinking about the unique feelings many of us have for our pets. In the abstract, I can't help but conclude that it is irrational to heap so much affection on an animal, particularly when human beings are in so much distress throughout the world. Maybe we do it because, like young children, they are totally dependent on us. But unlike children, who inevitably reach beyond us to another, more alluring world, our pets are forever bound to us by indestructible bonds of faith and comradeship. For them, there is no other world beyond the one we create, and in that there is an intoxicating security for both pet and owner.

W. H. Hudson

DEATH OF AN OLD DOG

When recalling the impressions and experiences of that most eventful sixth year, the one incident which looks biggest in memory, at all events in the last half of that year, is the death of Caesar. There is nothing in the past I can remember so well: it was indeed the most important event of my childhood—the first thing in a young life which brought the eternal note of sadness in.

It was in the early spring, about the middle of August, and I can even remember that it was windy weather and bitterly cold for the time of year, when the old dog was approaching his end.

Caesar was an old valued dog, although of no superior breed: he was just an ordinary dog of the country, short-haired, with long legs and a blunt muzzle. The ordinary dog or native cur was about the size of a Scotch collie; Caesar was quite a third larger, and it was said of him that he was as much above all other dogs of the house, numbering about twelve or fourteen, in intelligence and courage as in size. Naturally, he was the leader and master of the whole pack, and when he got up with an awful growl, baring his big teeth, and hurled himself on the others to chastise them for quarrelling or any other infringement of dog law, they took it lying down. He was a black dog, now in his old age sprinkled with white hairs all over his body, the face and legs having gone quite grey. Caesar in a rage, or on guard at night, or when driving cattle in from the plains, was a terrible being; with us children he was mild-tempered and patient, allowing us to ride on his back, just like old Pechicho the sheep-dog, described in the first chapter. Now, in his decline, he grew irritable and surly, and ceased to be our playmate. The last two or three months of his life were very sad, and when it troubled us to see him so gaunt, with his big ribs protruding from his sides, to watch his twitchings when he dozed, groaning and wheezing the while, and marked, too, how painfully he struggled to get up on his feet, we wanted to know why it was so—why we could not give him something to make him well? For answer they would open his great mouth to show us his teeth—the big blunt canines and old molars worn down to stumps. Old age was what ailed him—he was thirteen years old, and that did verily seem to me a great age, for I was not half that, yet it seemed to me that I had been a very, very long time in the world.

No one dreamed of such a thing as putting an end to him —no hint of such a thing was ever spoken. It was not the custom in that country to shoot an old dog because he was past work. I remember his last day, and how often we came to look at him and tried to comfort him with warm rugs and the offer of food and drink where he was lying in a sheltered place, no longer able to stand up. And that night he died: we knew it as soon as we were up in the morning. Then, after breakfast, during which we had been very solemn and quiet, our schoolmaster said: "We must bury him today—at twelve o'clock, when I am free, will be the best time; the boys can come with me, and old John can bring his spade." This announcement greatly excited us, for we had never seen a dog buried, and had never even heard of such a thing having ever been done.

About noon that day old Caesar, dead and stiff, was taken by one of the workmen to a green open spot among the old peach trees, where his grave had already been dug. We followed our schoolmaster and watched while the body was lowered and the red earth shovelled in. The grave was deep, and Mr. Trigg assisted in filling it, puffing very much over the task and stopping at intervals to mop his face with his coloured cotton handkerchief.

Then, when all was done, while we were still standing silently around, it came into Mr. Trigg's mind to improve the occasion. Assuming his schoolroom expression he looked round at us and said solemnly: "That's the end. Every dog has his day and so has every man; and the end is the same for both. We die like old Caesar, and are put into the ground and have the earth shovelled over us."

Now these simple, common words affected me more than any other words I have heard in my life. They pierced me to the heart. I had heard something terrible—too terrible to think of, incredible—and yet—and yet if it was not so, why had he said it? Was it because he hated us, just because we were children and he had to teach us our lessons, and wanted to torture us? Alas! no, I could not believe that! Was this, then, the horrible fate that awaited us all? I had heard of death—I knew there was such a thing; I knew that all animals had to die, also that some men died. For how could any one, even a child in its sixth year, overlook such a fact, especially in the country of my birth—a land of battle, murder, and sudden death? I had not forgotten the young man tied to the post in the barn who had killed some one, and would perhaps, I had been told, be killed himself as a punishment. I knew, in fact, that there was good and evil in the world, good and bad men, and the bad men—murderers, thieves, and liars—would all have to die, just like animals; but that there was any life after death I did not know. All the others, myself and my own people included, were good and would never taste death. How it came about that I had got no further in my system or philosophy of life I cannot say: I can only suppose that my mother had not yet begun to give me instruction in such matters on account of my tender years, or else that she had done so and that I had understood it in my own way. Yet, as I discovered later, she was a religious woman, and from infancy I had been taught to kneel and say a little prayer each evening: "Now I lay me down to sleep, I pray the Lord my soul to keep"; but who the Lord was or what my soul was I had no idea. It was just a pretty little way of saying in rhyme that I was going to bed.

My world was a purely material one, and a most wonderful world it was, but how I came to be in it I didn't know; I only knew (or imagined) that I would be in it always, seeing new and strange things every day, and never, never get tired of it. In literature it is only in Vaughan, Traherne, and other mystics, that I find any adequate expression of that perpetual rapturous delight in nature and my own existence which I experienced at that period.

And now these never-to-be-forgotten words spoken over the grave of our old dog had come to awaken me from that beautiful dream of perpetual joy!

W. H. Hudson

DANDY

He was of mixed breed, and was supposed to have a strain of Dandy Dinmont blood which gave him his name. A big ungainly animal with a rough shaggy coat of blue-gray hair and white on his neck and clumsy paws. He looked like a Sussex sheep dog with legs reduced to half their proper length. He was, when I first knew him, getting old and increasingly deaf and dim of sight, otherwise in the best of health and spirits, or at all events very good-tempered.

Until I knew Dandy I had always supposed that the story of Ludlam's dog was pure invention, and I dare say that is the general opinion about it; but Dandy made me reconsider the subject, and eventually I came to believe that Ludlam's dog did exist once upon a time, centuries ago perhaps, and that if he had been the laziest dog in the world Dandy was not far behind him in that respect. It is true he did not lean his head against a wall to bark; he exhibited his laziness in other ways. He barked often, though never at strangers; he welcomed every visitor, even the tax-collector, with tail-waggings and a smile. He spent a good deal of his time in the large kitchen, where he had a sofa to sleep on, and when the two cats of the house wanted an hour's rest they would coil themselves up on Dandy's broad shaggy side, preferring that bed to cushion or rug. They were like a warm blanket over him, and it was a sort of mutual benefit society. After an hour's sleep Dandy would go out for a short constitutional as far as the neighboring thoroughfare, where he would blunder against people, wag his tail to everybody, and then come back. He had six or eight or more outings each day, and, owing to doors and gates being closed and to his lazy disposition, he had much trouble in getting out and in. First he would sit down in the hall and bark, bark, bark, until some one would come to open the door for him, whereupon he would slowly waddle down the garden path, and if he found the gate closed he would again sit down and start barking. And the bark, bark would go on until some one came to let him out. But if after he had barked about twenty or thirty times no one came, he would deliberately open the gate himself, which he could do perfectly well, and let himself out. In twenty minutes or so he would be back at the gate and barking for admission once more, and finally, if no one paid any attention, letting himself in.

Dandy always had something to eat at meal-times, but he too liked a snack between meals once or twice a day. The dog-biscuits were kept in an open box on the lower dresser shelf, so that he could get one "whenever he felt so disposed," but he didn't like the trouble this arrangement gave him, so he would sit down and start barking, and as he had a bark which was both deep and loud, after it had been repeated a dozen times at intervals of five seconds, any person who happened to be in or near the kitchen was glad to give him his biscuit for the sake of peace and quietness. If no one gave it him, he would then take it out himself and eat it.

Now it came to pass that during the last year of the war dog-biscuits, like many other articles of food for man and beast, grew scarce, and were finally not to be had at all. At all events, that was what happened in Dandy's town of Penzance. He missed his biscuits greatly and often reminded us of it by barking; then, lest we should think he was barking about something else, he would go and sniff and paw at the empty box. He perhaps thought it was pure forgetfulness on the part of those of the house who went every morning to do the marketing and had fallen into the habit of returning without dog-biscuits in the basket. One day during that last winter of scarcity and anxiety I went to the kitchen and found the floor strewn all over with the fragments of Dandy's biscuit-box. Dandy himself had done it; he had dragged the box from its place out into the middle of the floor, and then deliberately set himself to bite and tear it into small pieces and scatter them about. He was caught at it just as he was finishing the job, and the kindly person who surprised him in the act suggested that the reason of his breaking up the box in that way was that he got something of the biscuit flavor by biting the pieces. My own theory was that as the box was there to hold biscuits and now held none, he had come to regard it as useless—as having lost its function, so to speak—also that its presence there was an insult to his intelligence, a constant temptation to make a fool of himself by visiting it half a dozen times a day only to find it empty as usual. Better, then, to get rid of it altogether, and no doubt when he did it he put a little temper into the business!

Dandy, from the time I first knew him, was strictly teetotal, but in former and distant days he had been rather fond of his glass. If a person held up a glass of beer before him, I was told, he wagged his tail in joyful anticipation, and a little beer was always given him at mealtime. Then he had an experience, which, after a little hesitation, I have thought it best to relate, as it is perhaps the most curious incident in Dandy's somewhat uneventful life.

One day Dandy, who after the manner of his kind, had attached himself to the person who was always willing to take him out for a stroll, followed his friend to a neighboring public-house, where the said friend had to discuss some business matter with the landlord. They went into the taproom, and Dandy, finding that the business was going to be a rather long affair, settled himself down to have a nap. Now it chanced that a barrel of beer which had just been broached had a leaky tap, and the landlord had set a basin on the floor to catch the waste. Dandy, waking from his nap and hearing the trickling sound, got up, and going to the basin quenched his thirst, after which he resumed his nap. By-and-by he woke again and had a second drink, and altogether he woke and had a drink five or six times; then, the business being concluded, they went out together, but no sooner were they out in the fresh air than Dandy began to exhibit signs of inebriation. He swerved from side to side, colliding with the passers-by, and finally fell off the pavement into the swift stream of water which at that point runs in the gutter at one side of the street. Getting out of the water, he started again, trying to keep close to the wall to save himself from another ducking. People looked curiously at him, and by-and-by they began to ask what the matter was. "Is your dog going to have a fit—or what is it?" they asked. Dandy's friend said he didn't know; something was the matter, no doubt, and he would take him home as quickly as possible and see to it.

When they finally got to the house Dandy staggered to the sofa, and succeeded in climbing on to it and, throwing himself on his cushion, went fast to sleep, and slept on without a break until the following morning. Then he rose quite refreshed and appeared to have forgotten all about it; but that day when at dinner-time some one said "Dandy" and held up a glass of beer, instead of wagging his tail as usual he dropped it between his legs and turned away in evident disgust. And from that time onward he would never touch it with his tongue, and it was plain that when they tried to tempt him, setting beer before him and smilingly inviting him to drink, he knew they were mocking him, and before turning away he would emit a low growl and show his teeth. It was the one thing that put him out and would make him angry with his friends and life companions.

I should not have related this incident if Dandy had been alive. But he is no longer with us. He was old—half-way between fifteen and sixteen: it seemed as though he had waited to see the end of the war, since no sooner was the armistice proclaimed than he began to decline rapidly. Gone deaf and blind, he still insisted on taking several constitutionals every day, and would bark as usual at the gate, and if no one came to let him out or admit him, he would open it for himself as before. This went on till January, 1919, when some of the boys he knew were coming back to Penzance and to the house. Then he established himself on his sofa, and we knew that his end was near, for there he would sleep all day and all night, declining food. It is customary in this country to chloroform a dog and give him a dose of strychnine to "put him out of his misery." But it was not necessary in this case, as he was not in misery; not a groan did he ever emit, waking or sleeping; and if you put a hand on him he would look up and wag his tail just to let you know that it was well with him. And in his sleep he passed away—a perfect case of euthanasia—and was buried in the large garden near the second apple-tree.

T. S. Eliot

LINES TO A YORKSHIRE TERRIER

In a brown field stood a tree
And the tree was crookt and dry.
In a black sky, from a green cloud
Natural forces shriek'd aloud,
Screamed, rattled, muttered endlessly.
Little dog was safe and warm
Under a cretonne eiderdown,
Yet the field was cracked and brown
And the tree was cramped and dry.
Pollicle dogs and cats all must
Jellicle cats and dogs all must
Like undertakers, come to dust.
Here a little dog I pause
Heaving up my prior paws,
Pause, and sleep endlessly.

Edward Carpenter

BRUNO

I cannot pass this period without dwelling on another friend, at that time a member of the household. I mean my dog Bruno—so-called, not from his color, for he was a very handsome black spaniel, but from some fanciful association with Giordano Bruno, the Italian. That dog—like so many black animals, black horses, black cats, black poodles, black-plumaged birds, rooks, jackadaws, starlings, and so forth—had something *demonic* about him. The tenderness and gentleness of his spirit, combined with a penetrative vision which searched one's very soul, was almost superhuman, I came first to know him when he was merely a puppy at a friend's house. We almost fell in love with each other then and there, and I was not altogether surprised when a few weeks afterwards he arrived at my door, sent on as a present from the said friends. He never doubted for a moment that he had come to his true home, and he settled down at once, a most loving member of the household. . . .

Bruno showed in high degree that curious quality resembling *conscience* in man, by which dogs, having contracted and adopted a new standard of life from their masters, betray an emotional conflict going on within them. Sometimes as is often the case where fowls are kept—we would have a nest of newly-hatched chicks being kept warm and dry in a basket on the hearth. On such occasions Bruno was torn by conflicting passions. The very sight and smell of the chicks roused the old primitive hunting instinct, and he would creep nearer and nearer to the basket in a very ecstasy of excitement—his limbs trembling and his nose quivering as he sniffed the prey. Yet he knew perfectly well that he must not touch; and his fidelity was so absolute that I firmly believe he harbored no intention of doing so. But who can tell? We felt that possibly a sudden frenzy of the animal nature might overtake him; and we could not do otherwise than keep on watch. As a matter of fact he never did do anything rash; but the tension on him, poor dog, was so great that sometimes for two or three days he would hardly touch his food, and he positively grew quite thin under the strain. It was really a relief for all of us when the hatching days were over.

There is something strangely touching in the fact that dogs not only thus develop a conscience foreign to their canine nature, but that also from their intentional devotion to their so-called "Masters" they are severed and alienated to some degree from the natural loves of their race—at any rate on the affectional side. I think Bruno nourished in his heart a strange susceptibility to beauty. His amours with other dogs were only of the ordinary kind; but he cherished for a certain white kitten a positive adoration. The kitten was certainly beautiful—snow-white and graceful to a degree—and to Bruno obviously a goddess; but alas! like other goddesses only too fickle and even cruel. When Bruno arrived on the scene, the kitten would skip on to the vantage point of a chair-seat; and from thence torment the pathetic and pleading nose of the dog with naughty scratches. Again and again would Bruno—wounded in his heart as well as in his head—return to his ineffectual suit, only to have his advances rejected as before. At last he had to abandon this quest, but it was curious that a year or two later he fell in love with *another* white kitten in much the same way and with much the same result.

"Everything comes to him who waits"; and the most curious and pathetic part of this story is its ending. For, a good many years afterwards when Bruno had become quite an old dog, and had lost much of his activity, a *cat* came and fell in love with him! This cat used to come from a neighboring farm and spend much of its time with the dog, and frequently at night would stay with him in the little outhouse which he used as a kennel, sleeping between the dog's paws. Ultimately the cat was there when Bruno died.

James Thurber

A SNAPSHOT OF REX

I ran across a dim photograph of him the other day, going through some old things. He's been dead about forty years. His name was Rex (my two brothers and I named him when we were in our early teens) and he was a bull terrier. "An American bull terrier," we used to say, proudly; none of your English bulls. He had one brindle eye that sometimes made him look like a clown and sometimes reminded you of a politician with derby hat and cigar. The rest of him was white except for a brindle saddle that always seemed to be slipping off and a brindle stocking on a hind leg. Nevertheless, there was a nobility about him. He was big and muscular and beautifully made. He never lost his dignity even when trying to accomplish the extravagant tasks my brothers and I used to set for him. One of these was the bringing of a ten-foot wooden rail into the yard through the back gate. We would throw it out into the alley and tell him to go get it. Rex was as powerful as a wrestler, and there were not many things that he couldn't manage somehow to get hold of with his great jaws and lift or drag to wherever he wanted to put them, or wherever we wanted them put. He would catch the rail at the balance and lift it clear of the ground and trot with great confidence toward the gate. Of course, since the gate was only four feet wide or so, he couldn't bring the rail in broadside. He found that out when he got a few terrific jolts, but he wouldn't give up. He finally figured out how to do it, by dragging the rail, holding onto one end, growling. He got a great, wagging satisfaction out of his work. We used to bet kids who had never seen Rex in action that he could catch a baseball thrown as high as they could throw it. He almost never let us down. Rex could hold a baseball with ease in his mouth, in one cheek, as if it were a chew of tobacco.

He was a tremendous fighter, but he never started fights. I don't believe he liked to get into them, despite the fact that he came from a line of fighters. He never went for another dog's throat but for one of its ears (that teaches a dog a lesson), and he would get his grip, close his eyes, and hold on. He could hold on for hours. His longest fight lasted from dusk until almost pitch-dark, one Sunday. It was fought in East Main Street in Columbus with a large, snarly non-descript that belonged to a big colored man. When Rex finally got his ear grip, the brief whirlwind of snarling turned to screeching. It was frightening to listen to and to watch. The Negro boldly picked the dogs up somehow and began swinging them around his head, and finally let them fly like a hammer in a hammer throw, but although they landed ten feet away with a great plump, Rex still held on.

The two dogs eventually worked their way to the middle of the car tracks, and after a while two or three streetcars were held up by the fight. A motorman tried to pry Rex's jaws open with a switch rod; somebody lighted a fire and made a torch of a stick and held that to Rex's tail, but he paid no attention. In the end, all the residents and storekeepers in the neighborhood were on hand, shouting this, suggesting that. Rex's joy of battle, when battle was joined, was almost tranquil. He had a kind of pleasant expression during fights, not a vicious one, his eyes closed in what would have seemed to be sleep had it not been for the turmoil of the struggle. The Oak Street Fire Department finally had to be sent for—I don't know why nobody thought of it sooner. Five or six pieces of apparatus arrived, followed by a battalion chief. A hose was attached and a powerful stream of water was turned on the dogs. Rex held on for several moments more while the torrent buffeted him about like a log in a freshet. He was a hundred yards away from where the fight started when he finally let go.

The story of that Homeric fight got all around town, and some of our relatives looked upon the incident as a blot on the family name. They insisted that we get rid of Rex, but we were very happy with him, and nobody could have made us give him up. We would have left town with him first, along any road there was to go. It would have been different, perhaps, if he had ever started fights, or looked for trouble. But he had a gentle disposition. He never bit a person in the ten strenuous years that he lived, nor ever growled at anyone except prowlers. He killed cats, that is true, but quickly and neatly and without especial malice, the way men kill certain animals. It was the only thing he did that we could never cure him of doing. He never killed or even chased a squirrel. I don't know why. He had his own philosophy about such things. He never ran barking after wagons or automobiles. He didn't seem to see the idea in pursuing something you couldn't catch, or something you couldn't do anything with, even if you did catch it. A wagon was one of the things he couldn't tug along with his mighty jaws, and he knew it. Wagons, therefore, were not a part of his world.

Swimming was his favorite recreation. The first time he ever saw a body of water (Alum Creek), he trotted nervously along the steep bank for a while, fell to barking wildly, and finally plunged in from a height of eight feet or more. I shall always remember that shining, virgin dive. Then he swam upstream and back just for the pleasure of it, like a man. It was fun to see him battle upstream against a stiff current, struggling and growling every foot of the way. He had as much fun in the water as any person I have known. You didn't have to throw a stick in the water to get him to go in. Of course, he would bring back a stick to you if you did throw one in. He would even have brought back a piano if you had thrown one in.

That reminds me of the night, way after midnight, when he went a-roving in the light of the moon and brought back a small chest of drawers that he had found somewhere—how far from the house nobody ever knew; since it was Rex, it could easily have been half a mile. There were no drawers in the chest when he got it home, and it wasn't a good one—he hadn't taken it out of anybody's house; it was just an old cheap piece that somebody had abandoned on a trash heap. Still, it was something he wanted, probably because it presented a nice problem in transportation. It tested his mettle. We first knew about his achievement when, deep in the night, we heard him trying to get the chest up onto the porch. It sounded as if two or three people were trying to tear the house down. We came downstairs and turned on the porch light. Rex was on the top step trying to pull the thing up, but it had caught somehow and he was just holding his own. I suppose he would have held his own till dawn if we hadn't helped him. The next day we carted the chest miles away and threw it out. If we had thrown it out in a near-by alley, he would have brought it home again, as a small token of his integrity in such matters. After all, he had been taught to carry heavy wooden objects about, and he was proud of his prowess.

I am glad Rex never saw a trained police dog jump. He was just an amateur jumper himself, but the most daring and tenacious I have ever seen. He would take on any fence we pointed out to him. Six feet was easy for him, and he could do eight by making a tremendous leap and hauling himself over finally by his paws, grunting and straining; but he lived and died without knowing that twelve- and sixteen-foot walls were too much for him. Frequently, after letting him try to go over one for a while, we would have to carry him home. He would never have given up trying.

There was in his world no such thing as the impossible. Even death couldn't beat him down. He died, it is true, but only as one of his admirers said, after "straight-arming the death angel" for more than an hour. Late one afternoon he wandered home, too slowly and too uncertainly to be the Rex that had trotted briskly homeward up our avenue for ten years. I think we all knew when he came through the gate that he was dying. He had apparently taken a terrible beating, probably from the owner of some dog that he had got into a fight with. His head and body were scarred. His heavy collar with the teeth marks of many a battle on it was awry; some of the big brass studs in it were sprung loose from the leather. He licked at our hands and, staggering, fell, but got up again. We could see that he was looking for someone. One of his three masters was not home. He did not get home for an hour. During that hour the bull terrier fought against death as he had fought against the cold, strong current of Alum Creek, as he had fought to climb twelve-foot walls. When the person he was waiting for did come through the gate, whistling, ceasing to whistle, Rex walked a few wobbly paces toward him, touched his hand with his muzzle, and fell down again. This time he didn't get up.

Michael J. Rosen

ANOTHER CHAIN

Unpacking a box of miscellaneous items in the garage, I come across Carey's collar, twenty-four inches of light chain with a cluster of charms—heart, fire hydrant, state of Ohio (ID, rabies, and registration tags). Carey was my first dog, a dog that lived with me and not my entire family. Carey was the puppy who chewed the spines of my college textbooks, the corners of my record albums, the letters dropped through the mail slot. Carey was the dog who taught me how many ways a twenty-year-old can fail a dog, despite whatever training love can muster. Carey was the aging dog my parents adopted when I went to graduate school, the dog who wouldn't leave my father's side while my father recuperated from each of his heart's damages. And when Carey's own body began its rapid deterioration, my father reminded us that Carey was the dog we owed a similar vigilance; and so we learned to administer the daily injection that kept him continent, helped the dog up and down the steps, in and out of the house, and offered Carey (our-selves?) a few more unanguished months together.

Automatically, as I do every day when I walk my present dogs, I slid the links of Carey's old collar through one of its end rings and formed a circle of chain. A straight line turned to a circle. And there it was: Carey's neck, restored in the perfunctory gesture.

Georgette LeBlanc-Maeterlinck
(Translated by Alexander Teixeira
de Mattos)

THE DEATH OF GOLAUD

The loss of our dear Golaud was a blow which I shall never forget. Unfortunately he did not die the easy death which his great virtues deserved. I shall always, when I think of it, ask myself certain melancholy questions. Had he still a glimmer of consciousness? Did he see anything, feel anything? Did he for a second fear the friendly hand which he had licked so often?

We know that dogs have only visions and that they do not think, because they do not speak; but, though they do not possess our mental power, is it fair to conclude that they possess none of any kind?

Between the visions presented by their little brains may there not be some relation the sense of which escapes us? It is certain that they love, that they do not love as we do, and —let us confess it—that they love better than we do, for their whole lives are at the service of their hearts.

Their love is blind, flawless, absolute and silent; it knows no doubt; and yet it is capable of suffering.

When we reflect that dogs have been known to die of grief, can we pretend that their darkness is without a single irradiating gleam? The instinct that leads them to find their lost master, an instinct which for us has something magical about it, since it renders them capable of accomplishing that which our understanding will never accomplish, are we to deny it all perspicacity? Must we conclude that it is wonderful only because it is quite unconscious and that our human love would have the same invincible power if it were not overshadowed by our loftier intelligence?

For months, Golaud's health had been failing. His increasingly short sight exposed him to all kinds of mishaps. One day he was discovered nearly drowned in the pond in which Adelaide committed suicide. He was continually stumbling and falling and colliding with things. Only a few precarious ties still bound him to his goddess, Habit. We had to begin thinking of how we should end his days. Our love for him became filled with anxiety. Would the kindest deliverance be a hypodermic injection of some poison or other? But chemists have been forbidden to sell poisons since the war. Any death not consecrated to the monster is apparently looked upon as a breach of the regulations.

Golaud is to die! They have laid him on a heap of cushions in the summer-house in the garden. He can no longer see nor hear nor smell; nevertheless he moans the moment I move away. How does he know that I am there?

I have placed a candle on the table; and I sit down beside our old friend and comrade. The cool of the evening enters through the broken panes.

Now and again he has a convulsive movement, which uncovers him; and his poor frame is revealed, all atremble. I keep on covering him up again and giving him water. His silence is a relief; and I am angry with myself for that very reason. Would he suffer more if he could tell me he was suffering?

Sometimes I find myself addressing him aloud:

"Yes, yes, my poor pet, you shall suffer no more after tonight, I promise you!"

I promise him death as the supreme comfort. I think of

the revolver which would bestow it upon him; and I am filled with loathing of our cowardice. . . .

Golaud is dead.

A kindly bullet has ended his dear little life.

Poor dog! Did he understand?

I have not been to look at him. I wanted to keep him in my memory alert, happy and assured of his own eternity; but the mournful picture is none the less in my mind; it pursues and hurts me.

I try to console myself, reflecting that no one ever scolded him and that his happiness was great.

What could be pleasanter than the life of a beloved dog? Our hurry to live alters our human destinies; we know that nothing lasts for ever; and this knowledge condemns in advance many things that come to life within us with imperishable energy. The dog, on the other hand, believes himself eternal; his perfect love is like himself; it is happy.

Golaud now lies at rest in the garden, in the shadow of a young mimosa-tree.

Sleep in peace, daddy dear, and let your jealousy be easy. There are new dogs in the house, but I shall not love them! You will be the last dog to find a place in my heart!

John Cheever

THE OLD DOG . . .
(From his Journals)

The old dog whimpers, cries in pain as she struggles to climb the stairs. She is the first one of us to grow old. In the twenty-five years that Mary and I have lived together we have known very little pain other than the pain of misunderstanding, childbirth, passing indebtedness, and head colds. We have, in fact, known very little in the way of change. We play the same games, walk the same distances, make love with the same frequency. When our parents were sick with age and dying, their care was never our responsibility. So the old bitch, her hindquarters crippled with rheumatism, is my first experience in the care of the infirm. I give her a boost from the rear and her cries of helplessness and misery are the cries of the old. These are the first sounds of real pain that this house, since it became ours, has heard.

The old dog; my love. That when we bought her someone pointed out that she was swaybacked and had a rib cage like a barrel. That as a young dog she was disobedient, greedy, and wicked. That she tipped over garbage pails, ripped wash off the clothesline, chewed up shoes of gold and silver, destroyed the babysitter's only spectacles, and refused to answer any commands; indeed, she seemed to laugh when she was called. She stole our clothing when we were clamming at Coskata, nearly drowned Mary in New Hampshire, and was a hazard on every beach. That she would retrieve a stick once or twice, but after that she would turn her back and pretend not to hear the command "Fetch." How we left her when we went to Europe, how she nibbled most of the upholstery, how when she heard my voice at the kennel she jumped a fence and hurled herself at me. That the introduction of love in our relationship came that day at Welton Falls. The stream was swollen and knocked her off her feet, and rolled her down a little falls into a pool. Then, when we returned, I hoisted her up in my arms and carried her over while she lapped my face. That with this her feelings toward me seemed to deepen. Her role as a confidante during some quarrelsome months. That my daughter, returning from school, would take her into the woods and pour into her ears her complaints about school, about her father and mother. Then it would be my turn, and then, after the dishes were washed, Mary's.

The difficulties with upholstered furniture. How she began in her middle age to dislike long walks. Starting up the beach for Coskata she would seem to enjoy herself, but if you took an eye off her she would swing around and gallop back to the house and her place in front of the fire. That she always got to her feet when I entered a room. That she enjoyed men very much and was conspicuously indifferent to women. That her dislikes were marked and she definitely preferred people from traditional and, if possible, wealthy origins. That she had begun to resemble those imperious and somehow mannish women who devilled my youth: the dancing teacher, the banker's wife, the headmistress of the progressive school I attended. There was a genre of imperious women in the twenties whose hell-for-leather manner made them seem slightly mannish. They were sometimes beautiful, but their airs were predatory and their voices were sometimes quite guttural. The time Susie put her off the jeep and she tried to commit suicide. How when I was alone and heard her wandering through the house my feelings for her were of love and gratitude; that her heavy step put me to sleep. Her difficulties in being photographed. That she barked when I talked loudly to myself. The book-review photograph, her figure arched with greed; the cigarette endorsement in which only her backside could be seen.

(And from a letter to Tanya Litvinov, his friend and Russian translator)

The old dog is dead. (This is the sort of news that will galvanize the mail-thief.) She lost the use of her legs on Sunday and her wits on Monday and I had the vet kill her yesterday afternoon. She was a wonderful companion and I loved her dearly but I shed very few tears. Fred cried for about an hour. We had her for fifteen years and she led a very active and useful life but when I took her for a walk she fell in the deep snow and had to be carried home. Some years ago I went to a psychiatrist who told me I was obsessed with my Mother. When I told him that I like to swim he said: Mother. When I told him that I liked the rain he said: Mother. When I told him that I drank too much he said: Mother. This was all rubbish but sitting here with Cassie one evening I saw her raise her head exactly as Mother used to and give me a pained, sweet, fleeting smile that was unnerving.

E. J. Kahn, Jr.

REPOSITORIES OF CONFIDENCE

January 1, 1977

It seemed like a good time of life, if perhaps a bit late, to start keeping a diary. When I see what I am thinking about in writing, I may be convinced it is true.

I started keeping a diary once before, in 1969, the painful, eventful year during which I was divorced from Jinny, married to Ellie, and separated from N. I stopped a month later, partly because Ellie said a diary, or journal, or whatever that was and this is, has to be something you can hide. I don't like secrets. In lieu of a diary, I was wont, in my first marital incarnation, to hold long private talks—rather, of course, monologues—with my Labrador retriever, Barge. A Labrador is an ideal vehicle for the repository of confidences, being large, warm, soft, patient, and taciturn. E. says one should use a diary the way one might, in other circumstances, use a Labrador retriever. She keeps her own diary, a conventional handwritten one, concealed beneath other unmentionables in a dresser drawer. I have read some of it. If I intended this to be an utterly secret diary, I would entrust to it my reaction to hers, but I have not even discussed that with Rainbow, our incumbent house pet, who is a cross between a Border collie and a Belgian shepherd.

Rainbow was given her name by Lexy, my younger stepson, when he was eleven, for no ascertainable reason, inasmuch as she, like Barge, and like New Zealand athletic teams, is all black. Sometimes when I am bemused or have drunk too much I call Rainbow "Barge." Sometimes, when it comes to that, I call Ellie "Jinny." I suppose after a twenty-four-year first marriage and a second one of only eight to date, that sort of thing is bound to happen occasionally.

February 7

E. swore when we were first married that among the things she would and would not do, a major Would Not would be having a dog in the city. I swore I would have only a Labrador retriever. . . . We compromised, which is the secret of success in any relationship, and we acquired a miniature dachshund. That did not work out especially well, because Jelly Bean was too fragile to withstand the wear and tear of being handled by two small boys. Out of compassion for the little dog's feelings, we gave him to a mature friend, which failed dramatically to improve Jelly Bean's lot; the friend inadvertently ran over him with her car. Rainbow, though a mongrel, is at least the size of a Labrador retriever, and, like most Labradors, she is all-black. Why, then, her multi-colored name? Why not indulge the imaginative whim of the eleven-year-old apprentice magician who brought her home? Why use adult criteria and question the nomenclatural judgment of a child when, after all, one sheeplike lets the same child's undeveloped tastes lead one time and time again to Howard Johnson's? Why isn't "Rainbow" every bit as good a name for a dog as "Jelly Bean"?

Barge was all-black, too, and unlike poor mixed-bred Rainbow, was a member in good, purebred standing of the American Kennel Club. Our beloved Cleopatra gave birth to Royal Barge of Holbrook, at Scarborough, roughly twenty-five years ago, on what was also my birthday. There was a party planned for me that night (I always say I don't want any fuss, but like most men I sure love to have a fuss), and inasmuch as Larry Adler was to be among the guests, that meant we had to get the piano tuned. If you expect a musical genius to preside over the singing of "Happy Birthday," you had better damn well have your ivories shipshape. The piano tuner misunderstood the directions to our house, and didn't arrive until 8 P.M., concurrent with the first guests.

He was still lying supine underneath the grand, with Larry instructing him from above, when Cleo began letting me know that she was going to have her puppies and to have them not in the elegant whelping room we had created for her downstairs but upstairs in the master bedroom. The first of her litter of nine emerged at 9 P.M. I had never before officiated as a veterinarian-obstetrician; but during the ensuing five hours I came to have new respect for both professions. (Also for the beautifully tidy way in which dogs dispose of afterbirths.) It was 2 A.M. before I got downstairs to greet those of my guests who were still around—the piano tuner, as I recall, among them—but most were kind enough, at one point or another in the evening, to come upstairs and give me a hand, although in truth Cleo did most of the really dirty work herself.

Barge, who helped Jinny and me raise our children, lived to be twelve. For the last year or so, he was not well. He had a heart attack and a stroke and from time to time could barely use his rear legs. When he went upstairs to bed (no self-respecting dog would sleep anywhere but in the master bedroom, and no self-respecting dog-owner would wish otherwise), I would have to carry his hindquarters. At Truro, one bitter-cold Thanksgiving weekend, he got outside one night, managed to propel himself to a favorite drainage ditch of his in a poison-ivy swamp, fell in, and couldn't climb out. Eventually we tracked him down by his barking, dragged him clear, got him back to the house, and scrubbed the mud off him and then off us. When it became apparent that for his own sake he had to be put away, I just couldn't be a party to it, and cravenly let Jinny drive him to Dr. Grossman's for the *coup de grâce*. To the bitter end, Barge was the best possible confidant and companion, and every bit as good a watchdog as Rainbow is today. Barge's terminal bark was, though, in a very literal sense, worse than his bite: Had an intruder violated our home, Barge would have roared at him but would have been unable to get to his feet and take any further punitive action. I was once going to write a short story about Barge's old age. The first sentence was to have been, "The burglar didn't know the dog was paralyzed." But I never could get beyond that without breaking down.

Glenn Matthew White

TOODLES DOESN'T UNDERSTAND

Our dog is dead. My wife and I have sworn we will not be sentimental about his demise and of course we are not. He knew a lot of happiness and he gave a lot. He lived a long life for a dog—nearly fourteen years—and he never had a sullen day. He came to live with us on our first wedding anniversary, so his lifetime spanned what were surely the most exciting, and maybe the best, years of our lives.

Our dog was scraped out of a sand hole full of mongrel puppies by a mower on a naval airfield when the hot war was our way of life. We named him Captain, for even as a white-and-tan ball of fluff, with his pointed black ears and vertical tail he was one of the lords of the earth. He never changed his attitude. Cap's vibrant spirit did not succumb to old age; he was alert and loyal to death. His courage and energy were just too great for his small body to contain any longer. His heart wore out from years of joyous beating.

Cap was an established member of our family when our first son was born, and virtually in charge when the second came. The boys liked him, but he was always our dog, never theirs. He was not a dog to be mauled, and he would bark sharply if any child tried it. Our boys treated him like an adult worthy of respect. They said "Excuse me, Cap," if they accidentally stepped on his proud plume of a tail. They meant it too. They are hardly so polite to their parents.

Without a doubt, Cap understood every word in the English language in ordinary use, and a good many common only in naval parlance. He would respond to conversation that he overheard while pretending to be asleep, and he knew the meaning of many words that we spelled out to fool him. We often kidded him for not learning how to talk—much to his discomfiture. He frequently tried, but never quite made it.

Cap traveled many thousands of miles with our family. He always knew when we were planning a trip and would patiently wait for us at the door of the car. For several months, when I was in a hospital, he stayed unleashed with the car, sleeping on top of it. He could get inside, but no stranger could.

His favorite sport was swimming; he would plunge fearlessly into roaring surf to fetch a stick. He had a purpose in life that he never doubted. In his lifetime, he must have fetched tens of thousands of sticks. He brought to our door anything of interest that he found in the trash. He brought to our bedside the newspaper that told of Hiroshima. One Christmas morning, after we had opened all the presents, he returned from a stroll with an expensive pair of new pigskin gloves in his mouth. I still wear them. We inquired about the neighborhood, but I don't think he stole them. I believe he bought them with his own money.

So he was a smart dog, a genius among mongrels, no less. Many people have loved such animals; many others think that to profess love for a dog is cloying and silly. My feeling is that any sort of love is better not discussed in public, and I would not be writing this eulogy if it were not for Toodles.

Toodles is a king-size blue-roan-and-tan English cocker with a pedigree going back six generations, and he is a guest in our house while his mistress travels abroad. After Cap's death, in family conclave we decided not to get another dog soon, if ever, but we were glad to take Toodles as a temporary boarder to see if our decision was wrong. Toodles has black silk ears six inches long, big soft jowls, doleful brown eyes. He is sad. He suffers from some nameless ancestral sorrow. If you gaze steadily at him for a while, you will feel your own ears growing longer, your eyes melting.

You will feel there is really no purpose in life, but we must all be brave.

We did not expect to find another dog as brilliant as Cap, but after Toodles had chewed up three hats, destroyed several pairs of my wife's hosiery, overturned a glass-topped lamp table, stolen a leg of lamb from the dinner table and scratched a large gash in the kitchen door, we were forced to conclude that, for a two-year-old, he was more than a little retarded. He will not "stay," he will not "bring," he will not "come." When called, he runs rapidly in the opposite direction. No, Cap was never guilty of such behavior, not even as a puppy. He would have been astonished, as we were, to find Toodles asleep on the kitchen table.

Cap was a fastidious eater and never gulped his food. It was his habit to let his food stand and nibble on it at his leisure. He would rarely eat anything but meat; if given a bone, he held it firmly upright between his paws and gnawed from the top down, neatly, and with delicacy. Toodles is a fur-covered maw and will gobble anything, including radishes, potato peelings, carrot tops and cellophane. He gnaws a bone by sprawling flat on the floor, bracing his paws wide apart and holding his head sideways. He prefers to eat it on the rug, where it doesn't slip so much. He has trouble with his long ears: they dangle into his food; they flop into his mouth and he chews on them.

Cap rarely wanted to be petted, and when he did he carefully rested his nose on my knee. Toodles' idea of affection is to leap on me when I'm napping, plant his huge paws on my eyeballs and drool in my face.

But Toodles is a good dog, pathetically eager to please. His intelligence quotient may be low, but he is a fawning, gurgling vibrator when petted or praised. He is sorry he is a dog. He is constantly apologetic and trembles with pleasure if he is forgiven. And he is brave. He barks at every odd sound he hears and some that he only imagines in the quiet of the night. He is a natural clown and often makes us laugh. The boys love him. He understands them.

It's the adults in the family that he doesn't understand. Toodles' owner will return to claim him soon, and the mistress of our house will surely miss him—not so much as the children will, but quite enough. He is not our dog. Our dog went yipping over the hill with a good bit of our youth and we shall never see his like again. Perhaps it is not Cap we mourn so much as the bright years he held together on a single, unbroken thread. For what can Toodles know of our pre-child home? How can any Toodles comprehend what life was like when love was new, before the hydrogen bomb, television and jet propulsion?

I add the moral for our sons: there are no second first times. First loves can never be repeated. If it is true that all a man needs for happiness is honest work, one good wife and some good dog, it's the better part of wisdom to know when he has them. Cap would understand. Cap knows all the secrets of our love and he keeps them well.

Ros and Mary Howard

SANDY IS GONE

Every kennel has a "number one" dog. Sometimes this is a
great show-dog. Now and then this is a dog who has never
seen a show-ring. And that's the way it was with Sandy.
She was a small, nicely-marked orange belton English setter. One of seven pups from a top-notch female's first litter.
Sandy had come home half-in, half-out of my jacket pocket
at barely five weeks.

Oh, I had big plans for Sandy. I had it all figured out:
combining English Shiplake and Canadian-Arthurlie blood-
lines as she did, I was going to breed her to Max; the great
son of Rumney Stagboro—who had only a few weeks before
gone Best in Show at Morris and Essex. Of course, she had
a while to grow and develop; and in the meantime she'd be
given a chance at the shows. Yes sir, I told myself, as I
looked at this beautiful headed tiny pup, it's all set!

And just to show you how wrong a breeder can be, every
single thing I planned for Sandy failed completely. And as it
turned out, she wasn't even my dog! She preferred Mary.

And she developed so many faults that I never did show
her. And because of this, and because this was still the depression, she was never bred to Max. (Sandy's dam was,
and produced several champions; and the lovely Southern
Lady of Aragon carried on from this line.)

Surprising to me, Sandy became, when finally given a chance, an excellent gun-dog.

Most important of all, Sandy became a touchstone for those depression years; the long, grim, war years, and this post-war period. Right from the start, she simply took over that number-one spot and occupied it with considerable dignity all of her life.

Her only vice was a craving for a cheap and inferior brand of canned dog food. Past the puppy stage, she would eat nothing else. Veterinaries said she couldn't live. Other breeders predicted an early death, scanty coat, and skin trouble. So, she thrived on this product, refused all other food; grew a beautiful coat, and developed a nasty skin rash when in desperation I force-fed her good lean horse meat!

Yes; Sandy surely was always a contradiction. When people would stop in at the kennel Sandy would greet them politely and escort them around to the runs where, from time to time there were beautiful pups. She would not only invite comparison, but insist on it by posing herself beside the dog a visitor was setting up. "Take a look at a real one!" she seemed to be saying; and there was never any shaking her confidence and high regard for her brains and her beauty. And admittedly, she was the smartest and sweetest setter I ever owned. Technically, her straight shoulder, her light bone, bad feet, and shoulder height of barely twenty-three inches made her unacceptable to my standards for a show setter. But that lovely head, and those dark eyes, and her dog wisdom and understanding more than made up for these artificial deficiencies.

From hiking in the hills and riding the waves in the Pacific coast to the confines of a tiny apartment in Cambridge, and on to a month's canoe trip in Northern Wisconsin, Sandy was always close beside us. No hotel ever refused Sandy; and she charmed more than one landlady with an admitted distaste for dogs! Invariably each said: Sandy is different. And I agreed, for when on her best behavior she could appear as nice as any well-bred young lady fresh from a proper finishing school. And Sandy always seemed to know exactly when to turn on this pose of dignity, polite interest and charm; and when to let go and become the happy hoyden she was at heart. I was proud of her on many occasions, but most of all I remember one late afternoon along in Fall, when clad as usual in sweat pants, sweat shirt and heavy sweater, I took Sandy for her daily road work of two miles along the Charles River. That year a younger brother was playing on the freshman football team at Harvard, and I always took a "break" and watched practice for a few minutes. This afternoon while we were taking our "break," a huge black limousine drew up across the road. The chauffeur climbed out and took a brace of handsome Springers from the car. And then an elderly and very dignified gentleman made his appearance from the rear seat. As Sandy and I watched, this gentleman unsnapped the leads and signalled the dogs to go. They covered the ground nicely; chased a squirrel up a tree, and in a minute or two returned on command. Again they were told to "find a bird!"

Sandy was very much interested; and after a minute or two we crossed the road and admired the dogs.

"The very finest Springers in Canada," we were told. "Finished gun-dogs, and of course bench champions." And after a monologue which carried us back to the sixth generation on one of these handsome dogs, Sandy was suddenly noticed. She had decided to sit, and was openly yawning in boredom.

"That's a, uh—nice looking setter you have," the gentleman said. "She is a setter, isn't she?" he added, thus letting us know his loose use of the word "nice."

And now Sandy proudly stood. Always the contradiction, she carried a beautifully full coat in July, and now in November she had not a hair over two inches on her tail, and no feathering at all on her legs!

We both looked at Sandy. She looked me right in the eye, and I didn't dare apologize for her. "She's the smartest setter I've ever owned," I said emphatically, and Sandy's tail wagged gayly in appreciation.

"More field type than bench," he said. "I imagine she's fine on pheasant."

I looked at Sandy, blaming her for this; but she was

blithely unaware of what her show-off posing had brought on.

"Pretty fair," I said, at the same time trying to imply modestly that she'd give Beau Essing a run for his money any time.

The chauffeur snapped the leads on the Springers and took them to the car.

"No birds here," the gentleman said emphatically. "It was really too much to expect; but if there had been one within a mile, those dogs would have found it. They never miss!"

Suddenly Sandy danced on her check-line, demanding to go.

"Why don't you let her go?"

And so, forced again by Sandy, I unsnapped the line. "Find 'em, girl," I told her, and racing like a shot thirty yards, she hit a stylish point and held it!

The owner of the Springers had quite a laugh over this. "Oh, a pretty point; but on nothing at all," he said.

And still Sandy held! On a hunch, I steadied her; moved past her—and flushed a cock and two hen pheasants!

"She's pretty fair," I repeated modestly as the owner of the "great" Springers retreated to his limousine.

Yes, Sandy's ways were always her own. And when she grew older, her favorite place was a high-backed old rocking chair, in which, proudly ensconced like a little old lady, she enjoyed nothing so much as a gentle rock two or three times a day, smartly balancing and controlling the rocking motion until she put herself to sleep for her more frequent naps now that she was getting on in years.

Dogs came and went; stayed and won at shows, produced litters; became grandfathers and grandmothers. And Sandy tolerated all of them, became intimate with none; detested all of the puppies; and now stayed constantly with Mary, sleeping on the foot of her bed.

From five weeks to old age, the "number one" dog in the kennel; but always living in the house. A lovable and affectionate setter, and with more good sense and judgment than any dog who ever owned us.

The war came along and Sandy stood on the front porch beside Mary when I left. She barked when I was a half a block away, and looking back I saw that she had moved closer to Mary.

And what a homecoming reception was waiting for me when I came back and ran up the steps! The old rocking chair going wildly and Sandy, dignity and restraint abandoned, jumping up into my arms and barking as I'd never heard her bark. And for the next week she accompanied me everywhere. And then I took her hunting and she really delivered the goods!

The kennel was built up; and pointers and setters came in from the East and Middlewest. Now Sandy retired to her rocking chair; moving from it only to take a short "constitutional" morning and afternoon; and barking when her chair was not in the sunshine.

Her lovely dark eyes had dimmed, her legs gone stiff, and her hearing was slowly fading; but her spirits were always high, and she was, at the last as from the first, "number one" of all our dogs; and in our hearts, too.

Robert Creeley

"HEY, SPOT!"

If you saw
dog pass, in car—

looking out, possibly
indifferently, at you—

would you—*could* you—
shout, "Hey, Spot!

It's me!" After all
these years,

no dog's coming home
again. Its skin's

moldered
through rain, dirt,

to dust, hair alone
survives, matted tangle.

Your own, changed,
your hair, greyed,

your voice not the one
used to call him home,

"Hey Spot!" *The world's
greatest dog's* got

lost in the world,
got lost long ago.

E. B. White

BEDFELLOWS

Turtle Bay, February 6, 1956

I am lying here in my private sick bay on the east side of town between Second and Third avenues, watching starlings from the vantage point of bed. Three Democrats are in bed with me: Harry Truman (in a stale copy of the *Times)*, Adlai Stevenson (in *Harper's)*, and Dean Acheson (in a book called *A Democrat Looks at His Party)*. I take Democrats to bed with me for lack of a dachshund, although as a matter of fact on occasions like this I am almost certain to be visited by the ghost of Fred, my dash-hound everlasting, dead these many years. In life, Fred always attended the sick, climbing right into bed with the patient like some lecherous old physician, and making a bad situation worse. All this dark morning I have reluctantly entertained him upon the rumpled blanket, felt his oppressive weight, and heard his fraudulent report. He was an uncomfortable bedmate when alive; death has worked little improvement—I still feel crowded, still wonder why I put up with his natural rudeness and his pretensions.

The only thing I used to find agreeable about him in bed was his smell, which for some reason was nonirritating to my nose and evocative to my mind, somewhat in the way that a sudden whiff of the cow barn or of bone meal on a lawn in springtime carries sensations of the richness of earth and of experience. Fred's aroma has not deserted him; it wafts over me now, as though I had just removed the stopper from a vial of cheap perfume. His aroma has not deserted the last collar he wore, either. I ran across this great, studded strap not long ago when I was rummaging in a cabinet. I raised it cautiously toward my nose, fearing a quill stab from his last porcupine. The collar was extremely high—had lost hardly 10 percent of its potency.

Fred was sold to me for a dachshund, but I was in a buying mood and would have bought the puppy if the storekeeper had said he was an Irish Wolfschmidt. He was only a few weeks old when I closed the deal, and he was in real trouble. In no time at all, his troubles cleared up and mine began. Thirteen years later he died, and by rights *my* troubles should have cleared up. But I can't say they have. Here I am, seven years after his death, still sharing a fever bed with him and, what is infinitely more burdensome, still feeling the compulsion to write about him. I sometimes suspect that subconsciously I'm trying to revenge myself by turning him to account, and thus recompensing myself for the time and money he cost me.

He was red and low-posted and long-bodied like a dachshund, and when you glanced casually at him he certainly gave the quick impression of being a dachshund. But if you went at him with a tape measure, and forced him onto scales, the dachshund theory collapsed. The papers that came with him were produced hurriedly and in an illicit atmosphere in a back room of the pet shop, and are most unconvincing. However, I have no reason to unsettle the Kennel Club; the fraud, if indeed it was a fraud, was ended in 1948, at the time of his death. So much of his life was given to shady practices, it is only fitting that his pedigree should have been (as I believe it was) a forgery.

I have been languishing here, looking out at the lovely branches of the plane tree in the sky above our city back yard. Only starlings and house sparrows are in view at this season, but soon other birds will show up. (Why, by the way, doesn't the *Times* publish an "Arrival of Birds" column, similar to its famous "Arrival of Buyers"?) Fred was a window gazer and bird watcher, particularly during his later years, when hardened arteries slowed him up and made it necessary for him to substitute sedentary pleasures for active sport. I think of him as he used to look on our bed in Maine—an old four-poster, too high from the floor for him to reach unassisted. Whenever the bed was occupied during the daylight hours, whether because one of us was sick or was napping, Fred would appear in the doorway and enter without knocking. On his big gray face would be a look of quiet amusement (at having caught somebody in bed during the daytime) coupled with his usual look of fake respectability. Whoever occupied the bed would reach down, seize him by the loose folds of his thick neck, and haul him painfully up. He dreaded this maneuver, and so did the occupant of the bed. There was far too much dead weight involved for anybody's comfort. But Fred was always willing to put up with being hoisted in order to gain the happy heights, as, indeed, he was willing to put up with far greater discomforts—such as a mouthful of porcupine quills —when there was some prize at the end.

Once up, he settled into his pose of bird watching, propped luxuriously against a pillow, as close as he could get to the window, his great soft brown eyes alight with expectation and scientific knowledge. He seemed never to tire of his work. He watched steadily and managed to give the impression that he was a secret agent of the Department of Justice. Spotting a flicker or a starling on the wing, he would turn and make a quick report.

"I just saw an eagle go by," he would say. "It was carrying a baby."

This was not precisely a lie. Fred was like a child in many ways, and sought always to blow things up to proportions that satisfied his imagination and his love of adventure. He was the Cecil B. deMille of dogs. He was a zealot, and I have just been reminded of him by a quote from one of the Democrats sharing my bed—Acheson quoting Brandeis. "The greatest dangers to liberty," said Mr. Brandeis, "lurk in insidious encroachment by men of zeal, well-meaning but without understanding." Fred saw in every bird, every squirrel, every housefly, every rat, every skunk, every porcupine, a security risk and a present danger to his republic. He had a dossier on almost every living creature, as well as on several inanimate objects, including my son's football.

Although birds fascinated him, his real hope as he watched the big shade trees outside the window was that a red squirrel would show up. When he sighted a squirrel, Fred would straighten up from his pillow, tense his frame, and then, in a moment or two, begin to tremble. The knuckles of his big forelegs, unstable from old age, would seem to go into spasm, and he would sit there with his eyes glued on the squirrel and his front legs alternately collapsing under him and bearing his weight again.

I find it difficult to convey the peculiar character of this ignoble old vigilante, my late and sometimes lamented companion. What was there about him so different from the many other dogs I've owned that he keeps recurring and does not, in fact, seem really dead at all? My wife used to claim that Fred was deeply devoted to me, and in a certain sense he was, but his was the devotion of an opportunist. He knew that on the farm I took the overall view and traveled pluckily from one trouble spot to the next. He dearly loved this type of work. It was not his habit to tag along faithfully behind me, as a collie might, giving moral support and sometimes real support. He ran a trouble-shooting business of his own and was usually at the scene ahead of me, compounding the trouble and shooting in the air. The word "faithful" is an adjective I simply never thought of in connection with Fred. He differed from most dogs in that he tended to knock down, rather than build up, the master's ego. Once he had outgrown the capers of puppyhood, he never again caressed me or anybody else during his life. The only time he was ever discovered in an attitude that suggested affection was when I was in the driver's seat of our car and he would lay his heavy head on my right knee. This, I soon perceived, was not affection, it was nausea. Drooling always followed, and the whole thing was extremely inconvenient, because the weight of his head made me press too hard on the accelerator.

Fred devoted his life to deflating me and succeeded admirably. His attachment to our establishment, though untinged with affection, was strong nevertheless, and vibrant. It was simply that he found in our persons, in our activities, the sort of complex, disorderly society that fired his imagination and satisfied his need for tumult and his quest for truth. After he had subdued six or seven porcupines, we realized that his private war against porcupines was an expensive bore, so we took to tying him, making him fast to any tree or wheel or post or log that was at hand, to keep him from sneaking off into the woods. I think of him as always at the end of some outsize piece of rope. Fred's disgust at these confinements was great, but he improved his time, nonetheless, in a thousand small diversions. He never just lay and rested. Within the range of his tether, he continued to explore, dissect, botanize, conduct post-mortems, excavate, experiment, expropriate, savor, masticate, regurgitate. He had no contemplative life, but he held as a steady gleam the belief that under the commonplace stone and behind the unlikely piece of driftwood lay the stuff of high adventure and the opportunity to save the nation.

But to return to my other bedfellows, these quick Democrats. They are big, solid men, every one of them, and they have been busy writing and speaking, and sniffing out the truth. I did not deliberately pack my counterpane with members of a single political faith; they converged on me by the slick device of getting into print. All three turn up saying things that interest me, so I make bed space for them.

Mr. Truman, reminiscing in a recent issue of the *Times,* says the press sold out in 1948 to "the special interests," was 90 percent hostile to his candidacy, distorted facts, caused his low popularity rating at that period, and tried to prevent him from reaching the people with his message in the campaign. This bold, implausible statement engages my fancy because it is a half-truth, and all half-truths excite me. An attractive half-truth in bed with a man can disturb him as deeply as a cracker crumb. Being a second-string member of the press myself, and working, as I do, for the special interests, I tend to think there is a large dollop of pure irascibility in Mr. Truman's gloomy report. In 1948, Mr. Truman made a spirited whistle-stop trip and worked five times as hard as his rival. The "Republican-controlled press and radio" reported practically everything he said, and also gave vent to frequent horse-laughs in their editorials and commentaries. Millions of studious, worried Americans heard and read what he said; then they checked it against the editorials; then they walked silently into the voting booths and returned him to office. Then they listened to Kaltenborn. Then they listened to Truman doing Kaltenborn. The criticism of the opposition in 1948 was neither a bad thing nor a destructive thing. It was healthy and (in our sort of society) necessary. Without the press, radio, and TV, President Truman couldn't have got through to the people in anything like the volume he achieved. Some of the published news was distorted, but distortion is inherent in partisan journalism, the same as it is in political rallies. I have yet to see a piece of writing, political or non-political, that doesn't have a slant. All writing slants the way a writer leans, and no man is born perpendicular, although many men are born upright. The beauty of the American free press is that the slants and the twists and the distortions come from so many directions, and the special interests are so numerous, the reader must sift and sort and check and countercheck in order to find out what the score is. This he does. It is only when a press gets its twist from a single source, as in the case of government-controlled press systems, that the reader is licked.

Democrats do a lot of bellyaching about the press's being preponderantly Republican, which it is. But they don't do the one thing that could correct the situation: they don't go into the publishing business. Democrats say they haven't got that kind of money, but I'm afraid they haven't got that kind of temperament or, perhaps, nerve.

Adlai Stevenson takes a view of criticism almost opposite to Harry Truman's. Writing in *Harper's,* Stevenson says, ". . . I very well know that in many minds 'criticism' has today become an ugly word. It has become almost *lèse majesté.* It conjures up pictures of insidious radicals hacking away at the very foundations of the American way of life. It suggests nonconformity and nonconformity suggests disloyalty and disloyalty suggests treason, and before we know where we are, this process has all but identified the critic with the saboteur and turned political criticism into an un-American activity instead of democracy's greatest safeguard."

The above interests me because I agree with it and everyone is fascinated by what he agrees with. Especially when he is sick in bed.

Mr. Acheson, in his passionately partisan yet temperate book, writes at some length about the loyalty-security procedures that were started under the Democrats in 1947 and have modified our lives ever since. This theme interests me because I believe, with the author, that security declines as security machinery expands. The machinery calls for a secret police. At first, this device is used solely to protect us from unsuitable servants in sensitive positions. Then it broadens rapidly and permeates nonsensitive areas, and, finally, business and industry. It is in the portfolios of the secret police that nonconformity makes the subtle change into disloyalty. A secret-police system first unsettles, then desiccates, then calcifies a free society. I think the recent loyalty investigation of the press by the Eastland subcommittee was a disquieting event. It seemed to assume for Congress the right to poke about in newspaper offices and instruct the management as to which employees were okay and which were not. That sort of procedure opens wonderfully attractive vistas to legislators. If it becomes an accepted practice, it will lead to great abuses. Under extreme conditions, it could destroy the free press.

The loyalty theme also relates to Fred, who presses ever more heavily against me this morning. Fred was intensely loyal to himself, as every strong individualist must be. He held unshakable convictions, like Harry Truman. He was absolutely sure that he was in possession of the truth. Because he was loyal to himself, I found his eccentricities supportable. Actually, he contributed greatly to the general health and security of the household. Nothing has been quite the same since he departed. His views were largely of a dissenting nature. Yet in tearing us apart he somehow held us together. In obstructing, he strengthened us. In criticizing, he informed. In his rich, aromatic heresy, he nourished our faith. He was also a plain damned nuisance, I must not forget that.

The matter of "faith" has been in the papers again lately. President Eisenhower (I will now move over and welcome a Republican into bed, along with my other visitors) has come out for prayer and has emphasized that most Americans are motivated (as they surely are) by religious faith. The *Herald Tribune* headed the story, PRESIDENT SAYS PRAYER IS PART OF DEMOCRACY. The implication in such a pronouncement, emanating from the seat of government, is that religious faith is a *condition,* or even a *precondition,* of the democratic life. This is just wrong. A President should pray whenever and wherever he feels like it (most Presidents have prayed hard and long, and some of them in desperation and in agony), but I don't think a President should advertise prayer. That is a different thing. Democracy, if I understand it at all, is a society in which the unbeliever feels undisturbed and at home. If there were only half a dozen unbelievers in America, their well-being would be a test of our democracy, their tranquillity would be its proof. The repeated suggestion by the present administration that religious faith is a precondition of the American way of life is disturbing to me and, I am willing to bet, to a good many other citizens. President Eisenhower spoke of the tremendous favorable mail he received in response to his inaugural prayer in 1953. What he perhaps did not realize is that the persons who felt fidgety or disquieted about the matter were not likely to write in about it, lest they appear irreverent, irreligious, unfaithful, or even un-American. I remember the prayer very well. I didn't mind it, although I have never been able to pray electronically and doubt that I ever will be. Still, I was able to perceive that the President was sincere and was doing what came naturally, and anybody who is acting in a natural way is all right by me. I believe that our political leaders should live by faith and should, by deeds and sometimes by prayer, demonstrate faith, but I doubt that they should *advocate* faith, if only because such advocacy renders a few people uncomfortable. The concern of a democracy is that no honest man shall feel uncomfortable, I don't care who he is, or how nutty he is.

I hope that belief never is made to appear mandatory. One of our founders, in 1787, said, "Even the diseases of the people should be represented." Those were strange, noble words, and they have endured. They were on television yesterday. I distrust the slightest hint of a standard for political rectitude, knowing that it will open the way for persons in authority to set arbitrary standards of human behavior.

Fred was an unbeliever. He worshiped no personal God, no Supreme Being. He certainly did not worship *me*. If he had suddenly taken to worshiping me, I think I would have felt as queer as God must have felt the other day when a minister in California, pronouncing the invocation for a meeting of Democrats, said, "We believe Adlai Stevenson to be Thy choice for President of the United States. Amen."

I respected this quirk in Fred, this inability to conform to conventional canine standards of religious feeling. And in the miniature democracy that was, and is, our household he lived undisturbed and at peace with his conscience. I hope my country will never become an uncomfortable place for the unbeliever, as it could easily become if prayer was made one of the requirements of the accredited citizen. My wife, a spiritual but not a prayerful woman, read Mr. Eisenhower's call to prayer in the *Tribune* and said something I shall never forget. "Maybe it's all right," she said. "But for the first time in my life I'm beginning to feel like an outsider in my own land."

Democracy is itself a religious faith. For some it comes close to being the only formal religion they have. And so when I see the first faint shadow of orthodoxy sweep across the sky, feel the first cold whiff of its blinding fog steal in from sea, I tremble all over, as though I had just seen an eagle go by, carrying a baby.

Anyway, it's pleasant here in bed with all these friendly Democrats and Republicans, every one of them a dedicated man, with all these magazine and newspaper clippings, with Fred, watching the starlings against the wintry sky, and the prospect of another presidential year, with all its passions and its distortions and its dissents and its excesses and special interests. Fred died from a life of excesses, and I don't mind if I do, too. I love to read all these words—most of them sober, thoughtful words—from the steadily growing book of democracy: Acheson on security, Truman on the press, Eisenhower on faith, Stevenson on criticism, all writing away like sixty, all working to improve and save and maintain in good repair what was so marvelously constructed to begin with. This is the real thing. This is bedlam in bed. As Mr. Stevenson puts it: ". . . no civilization has ever had so haunting a sense of an ultimate order of goodness and rationality which can be known and achieved." It makes me eager to rise and meet the new day, as Fred used to rise to his, with the complete conviction that through vigilance and good works all porcupines, all cats, all skunks, all squirrels, all houseflies, all footballs, all evil birds in the sky could be successfully brought to account and the scene made safe and pleasant for the sensible individual—namely, him. However distorted was his crazy vision of the beautiful world, however perverse his scheme for establishing an order of goodness by murdering every creature that seemed to him bad, I had to hand him this: he really worked at it.

P.S. (June 1962). This piece about prayer and about Fred drew a heavy mail when it appeared—heavy for me, anyway. (I call six letters a heavy mail.) Some of the letters were from persons who felt as I did about the advocacy of prayer but who had been reluctant to say anything about it. And there were other letters from readers who complained that my delineation of Fred's character (half vigilante, half dissenter) was contradictory, or at least fuzzy. I guess there is some justification for this complaint: the thing didn't come out as clear as I would have liked, but nothing I write ever does.

In the 1960 presidential campaign, faith and prayer took a back seat and the big question was whether the White House could be occupied by a Catholic or whether that would be just too much. Again the voters studied the *Racing Form,* the *Wall Street Journal,* the *Christian Science Monitor;* they sifted the winds that blew through the Republican-controlled press; they gazed into television's crystal ball; they went to church and asked guidance; and finally they came up with the opinion that a Catholic *can* be President. It was a memorable time, a photo finish, and a healthful exercise generally.

The McCarthy era, so lately dead, has been followed by the Birch Society era (eras are growing shorter and shorter in America—some of them seem to last only a few days), and again we find ourselves with a group of people that proposes to establish a standard for political rectitude, again we have vigilantes busy compiling lists and deciding who is anti-Communist and who fails in that regard. Now in 1962, conservatism is the big, new correct thing, and the term "liberal" is a term of opprobrium. In the newspaper that arrives on my breakfast table every morning, liberals are usually referred to as "so-called" liberals, the implication being that they are probably something a whole lot worse than the name "liberal" would indicate, something really shady. The Birchers, luckily, are not in as good a position to create sensational newspaper headlines as was Senator McCarthy, who, because he was chairman of a Senate committee, managed to turn page one into a gibbet, and hung a new fellow each day, with the help of a press that sometimes seemed to me unnecessarily cooperative in donating its space for the celebration of those grim rites.

Prayer broke into the news again with the Supreme Court's decision in the New York school prayer case. From the violence of the reaction you would have thought the Court was in the business of stifling America's religious life and that the country was going to the dogs. But I think the Court again heard clearly the simple theme that ennobles our Constitution: that no one shall be made to feel uncomfortable or unsafe because of nonconformity. New York State, with the best intentions in the world, created a moment of gentle orthodoxy in public school life, and here and there a child was left out in the cold, bearing the stigma of being different. It is this one child that our Constitution is concerned about—his tranquillity, his health, his safety, his conscience. What a kindly old document it is, and how brightly it shines, through interpretation after interpretation!

One day last fall I wandered down through the orchard

and into the woods to pay a call at Fred's grave. The trees were bare; wild apples hung shamelessly from the grapevine that long ago took over the tree. The old dump, which is no longer used and which goes out of sight during the leafy months, lay exposed and candid—rusted pots and tin cans and sundries. The briers had lost some of their effectiveness, the air was good, and the little dingle, usually so mean and inconsiderable, seemed to have acquired stature. Fred's headstone, ordinarily in collapse, was bolt upright, and I wondered whether he had quieted down at last. I felt uneasy suddenly, as the quick do sometimes feel when in the presence of the dead, and my uneasiness went to my bladder. Instead of laying a wreath, I watered an alder and came away.

This grave is the only grave I visit with any regularity—in fact, it is the only grave I visit at all. I have relatives lying in cemeteries here and there around the country, but I do not feel any urge to return to them, and it strikes me as odd that I should return to the place where an old dog lies in a shabby bit of woodland next to a private dump. Besides being an easy trip (one for which I need make no preparation) it is a natural journey—I really go down there to see what's doing. (Fred himself used to scout the place every day when he was alive.) I do not experience grief when I am down there, nor do I pay tribute to the dead. I feel a sort of overall sadness that has nothing to do with the grave or its occupant. Often I feel extremely well in that rough cemetery, and sometimes flush a partridge. But I feel sadness at All Last Things, too, which is probably a purely selfish, or turned-in, emotion—sorrow not at my dog's death but at my own, which hasn't even occurred yet but which saddens me just to think about in such pleasant surroundings.

Robinson Jeffers

THE HOUSE-DOG'S GRAVE —
HAIG'S GRAVE

I've changed my ways a little: I cannot now
Run with you in the evenings along the shore,
Except in a kind of dream and you,
    if you dream a moment,
You see me there.

So leave awhile the paw-marks on the front door
Where I used to scratch to go out or in,
And you'd soon open; leave on the kitchen floor
The marks of my drinking-pan.

I cannot lie by your fire as I used to do
On the warm stone,
Nor at the foot of your bed: no, all the nights through
I lie alone.

But your kind thought has laid me less than six feet
Outside your window where firelight so often plays,
And where you sit to read—and I fear often
    grieving for me—
Every night your lamplight lies on my place.

You, man and woman, live so long it is hard
To think of you ever dying.
A little dog would get tired of living so long,
I hope that when you are lying

Under the ground like me your lives will appear
As good and joyful as mine.
No, dears, that's too much hope: you are not
    as well cared for
As I have been,

And never have known the passionate undivided
Fidelities that I knew.
Your minds are perhaps too active, too many-sided...
But to me you were true.

You were never masters but friends. I was your friend.
I loved you well, and was loved. Deep love endures
To the end and far past the end. If this is my end
I am not lonely. I am not afraid. I am still yours.

Albert R. Hunt

R.I.P. AMANDA, 1983-1994

Last month we lost a member of the family. Amanda passed away. She was our golden retriever, a month shy of 11 years old—or almost 77 in dog years.

The world can be divided into two types of people: animal lovers and others. The latter never will understand the grieving, the profound sense of loss, the huge void when a long-time pet dies.

For our three children this was the most immediate experience of dying they have known. Yet Amanda's final days served as a family catharsis. For all the sadness and tears, it was a great bonding experience; my wife and I discovered that our kids have strengths that we never fully appreciated.

Amanda was a looming presence in all our lives. She was a gift to Jeffrey, now 12 years old, on his second birthday. The two of them literally grew up together. She was at the door when his younger brother and then younger sister arrived home for the first time. Amanda was too sweet to ever moonlight as a watchdog, yet the children always thought her a comforting protector; she encouraged that ruse.

She was in the center of every festive occasion. At Christmas she reveled in her presents—often with more appreciation than the kids showed—although they always were the same sort of bones and rubber toys. She loved birthdays not merely because she always got some of the cake, though that was special. She just adored happy times.

Then there was Amanda the mother. Over 14 months she had two litters, 15 puppies. Both pregnancies were unplanned, but fortunately they were the result of a steady relationship with a boy of her own faith—a neighbor golden of Republican extraction named Winston. Our two boys, especially Jeffrey, saw her bring lives into this world and witnessed the marvelous nurturing instincts of a mother.

Most of all she was a constant companion and friend. On those days when my wife and I came home from work tired, frustrated or even angry, Amanda always was there with her tail wagging, a smile on her face, overjoyed that her family was together. When the children fought or were punished, Amanda always was there to console them. She taught us more than we realized, both about perspective and family. She gave us a rare commodity: unconditional love.

Over the final days, she also taught us a lot about how to die with grace, and how to deal with it. Days before she died, my brother, the world's most compassionate veterinarian, sent two books for the younger kids: "The Tenth Good Thing About Barney" by Judith Viorst, and "When a Pet Dies" by Fred Rogers of "Mr. Rogers' Neighborhood" fame. Anyone going through this trauma will find these books invaluable.

But it was her real master, Jeffrey, himself still months away from being a teenager, who had to struggle most valiantly with the realities of an imminent loss. Her kidneys had failed and she went downhill quickly. The only humane course was to put her to sleep, but Jeffrey wanted to bring her home for one last night. It could have been maudlin; it wasn't.

The next morning right before I took her to the veterinarian, he again told her how important she had been to him. Jeffrey's forte never has been sharing with siblings, but he then urged his younger brother and sister to tell her goodbye, too. Five-year-old Lauren had a final girl-to-girl talk with her. Then as we were about to drive away, Benjamin, age seven, kissed her on the head and softly said, "Bye-bye, Amanda, I'll see you in heaven."

Tom Stienstra

COPING WITH DEATH
OF A LOVED ONE

The biggest challenge I've ever known was trying to be the person my dog always thought I was.

When I first got my dog, I was lost like a piece of driftwood floating about the open sea. All I had was an old pickup truck, sleeping bag and a typewriter, and I was adrift, with no job and thin roots, wandering about the West, camping, hiking and fishing, wondering how I'd even pay for the gas for the next trip.

Then I got this dog, black mainly. Turned out he was just as lost as I was. In fact, if he wasn't claimed that day, he was headed for a permanent home in the sky. Back then a lot of people felt I was a walking time bomb, erratic and ornery. But right off, that dog loved me anyway, and suddenly, I had something to live up to. Some people said I "saved him," but it was always the other way around.

That was nearly 17 years ago. And last week, as I shoveled the last scoop of dirt on his grave, I felt the full force of the impact he had on my life, as well as how our personalities had become woven together as we roamed year after year on adventures across the land.

Many people who love their dogs or cats will understand.

As many review their lives, some automatically divide their memories into different eras according to the pets they have owned. You see, while many people are always passing in and out of your daily experiences, your dog stays. There is no animal more loyal, a creature with a rare tolerance for our many shortcomings.

Seventeen years ago, that black dog needed me so bad that he followed me everywhere, so I named him "Shadow." But the name didn't take. Then when he got left home alone one evening for a few hours, and proceeded to tear down several curtains in the house, my brother Bob said, "He's a reb," and the dog's ears perked up. So his name became Reb, then a week later, Rebel.

From that moment on, he became my 24-hour-a-day partner. I'd drive that pickup truck around, my buddy right with me all the time, then we'd get out and hike, camp or fish, making each day a discovery. Each morning, I would start the day by writing a story on that old typewriter, and that's when Rebel would curl up at my feet, asleep with his head on my boots, a habit he kept right up to the last day.

He could outrun a deer, outswim a duck, and outwit just about anything but a skunk, at least the first encounter with one anyway. One late evening at a Sierra camp, a bear strolled up and drank out of his water bowl, and Rebel faked sleeping through the whole affair. Smartest move I've ever seen. But just when you'd think you figured out his logic, he'd set out on some mission of individual craziness.

Once he crashed through ocean breakers and chased a sea lion a quarter mile out to sea, then swam back and body-surfed in to the beach. He loved taking flying leaps off ledges into ponds, then swimming for 30 or 40 minutes, chasing ducks around, sometimes even catching one. On one hike, he sniffed out a fawn that had fallen into a dry well shaft, 12 feet deep, jumped in right alongside—barked for my attention, and in the process rescued the deer by bringing me to the scene.

Rebel became such a happy, free spirit that he had almost a prance to his walk. Even as he neared 15, people were amazed at his physical condition and mental spark.

But Rebel's hearing became quite poor, though friends

noticed that he appeared to understand everything I said by watching my mouth. The strength in his legs began to wane, and I had a miniature staircase built so he could still climb into my truck. When I petted him, I began to notice his shoulder blades, that he was losing weight. But he was happy in his retirement, still full of spark, demanding play time and ride time in the truck, still sleeping on my boots every morning as I typed away, always managing to curl up on a corner of my sleeping bag at camps.

I know the price of living is dying, and you try to prepare yourself for the inevitable. But the shock when he had a stroke at my feet one morning, paralyzing him, was beyond anything I could have imagined.

After several hours talking with him, I put his head in my hands, rubbed that favorite spot on his forehead, and told him it was time for him to go to heaven. He gave me a lick on my cheek, aware of what was happening, and then the vet put him to sleep.

As I cupped his body in my arms, I felt adrift for the first time in 17 years, lost at sea without a heading, devastated and alone. A moment later, I sensed something rise from him, produce a profound sensation, hover for a moment, then suddenly vanish. His body then seemed empty, a shell.

Later, a friend clipped two blooming iris from the front yard and gave them to me, and I placed one in a vase on a table, the other on Rebel's burial site, set in a pristine forest that will always remain untouched. In two days, the iris in the vase wilted, the bloom withering to nothing. But 11 days later, the one on the grave was still fresh and blooming.

An Indian friend of mine, Dancing Water, said such things can be explained. "The flower in your house was a symbol of your loss," Dancing Water said. "The flower on the grave is a symbol of his spirit, which lives on. It is a message to you that he is where he belongs now, and for you too to now live on, to celebrate life as you know it, and live it fully again."

While there are two expeditions and several excursions awaiting, I find I keep looking for my old buddy, expecting him to suddenly come bounding along, just as he had thousands of time on our trips together.

But though he is not there, it is onward I must go. Over the years I have not only shared a friendship like no other, but in his passing, I have felt divine force, and I know there will come a day when we will meet again.

Anna Tuttle Villegas

SWEET DOG, GONE

For Tracker, Who Died in Thunderstorm,
Calaveras County

Ten childless years
Through and through
I owned you.
And owning so—a decade's lease—
Claimed certain knowledge:
Your love of water.
How you leaned into silence,
In silence finding sound.
Your curled weight cradled,
Hammocked between our bodies
Where we slept
With what was left us:
Tangled in two-legged vanity.

But I did not know,
Oh
How could I not have known,
That a day of thunder
Would shiver
Shrapnel
Shatter
You
Who leaned into silence
To find sound.

Did you feel I loved you best?
Forgive me now.
I did.
More than the setter tramp
Whose auburn coat caught foxtails
And earned him hours in my lap,
When you would lie
And watch my hands
Moving like a lover's,
Searching his sleek sides.

Every time he swallowed quills
And I locked his head between my knees
And cocked the pliers
And pulled,
You got no reward
For being smarter,
For staying close to home.
You leaned against his whimpered anger,
And waited,
And saw his dogteeth
Brush my skin.

When the baby came,
And the husband left, finally,
You I could trust,
Not the setter,
Who had snapped chains
To trespass, or do worse.
You never brought me my own geese
Tendrilled from your bloodfoamed mouth
Like trophies torn from my heart.
Even dying you did in silence
In bloodless black.

That morning
In cracking panes of rain
And bolted shards of sound—
The baby cried, too, I remember that—
I put you out.
You didn't want to go.
Rigid with human rules,
I pulled you
Into the weather,
Shut the door,
Didn't look back.

That night, home
To an empty house,
The woodstove cold,
The baby nursed, then sleeping,
I stoked the fire
And searched for *you*.
I called, I promise.
I walked,
You know I did.

The wind took your name
And turned it silent.
You weren't there
To be saved
By sound.

Jack Fischer brought you home.
"Feeding late," he said.
I smelled the cows on him
And watched his big hard hands
Tangle in your coat
As mine had done too seldom.
"Right off the shoulder,
Two miles up...doesn't
Seem like he should be dead...
No blood."

Against the breast
That nursed the baby,
That held the heart
That hardened the husband,
That failed to learn
Your fear of sound,
I clasped you.

Bareheaded, I buried you in rain,
Not penance enough
To stop my weeping.
I weep still.

The house dog now
Has your eyes.
They follow me.
They know my part.
Every crime that I've collected

Stands around your stone-starred grave
To bring home my wrongs.
In the cut of light
Cast from a cracked-wide sky,
I lean into silence
For sound.

Eugene O'Neill

THE LAST WILL AND TESTAMENT
OF SILVERDENE EMBLEM O'NEILL

I, Silverdene Emblem O'Neill (familiarly known to my family, friends and acquaintances as Blemie), because the burdens of my years and infirmities is heavy upon me, and I realize the end of my life is near, do hereby bury my last will and testament in the mind of my Master. He will not know it is there until after I am dead. Then, remembering me in his loneliness, he will suddenly know of this testament, and I ask him then to inscribe it as a memorial to me.

I have little in the way of material things to leave. Dogs are wiser than men. They do not set great store upon things. They do not waste their days hoarding property. They do not ruin their sleep worrying about how to keep the objects they have, and to obtain the objects they have not. There is nothing of value I have to bequeath except my love and my faith. These I leave to all those who have loved me, to my Master and Mistress, who I know will mourn me most, to Freeman who has been so good to me, to Cyn and Roy and Willie and Naomi.[1] But if I should list all those who have loved me it would force my Master to write a book. Perhaps it is vain of me to boast when I am so near

<hr>

[1] Hubert Freeman was O'Neill's chauffeur and man of all work, Cynthia and Roy Strain were Carlotta O'Neill's daughter by her first marriage and son-in-law, and Willie and Naomi Tompkins were the O'Neills' butler and cook.

death, which returns all beasts and vanities to dust, but I have always been an extremely lovable dog.

I ask my Master and Mistress to remember me always, but not to grieve for me too long. In my life I have tried to be a comfort to them in time of sorrow, and a reason for added joy in their happiness. It is painful for me to think that even in death I should cause them pain. Let them remember that while no dog has ever had a happier life (and this I owe to their love and care for me), now that I have grown blind and deaf and lame, and even my sense of smell fails me so that a rabbit could be right under my nose and I might not know, my pride has sunk to a sick, bewildering humiliation. I feel life is taunting me with having over-lingered my welcome. It is time I said goodbye, before I become too sick a burden on myself and on those who love me. It will be sorrow to leave them, but not a sorrow to die. Dogs do not fear death as men do. We accept it as a part of life, not as something alien and terrible which destroys life. What may come after death, who knows? I would like to believe with those of my fellow Dalmatians who are devout Mohammedans, that there is a Paradise where one is always young and full-bladdered; where all the day one dillies and dallies with an amorous multitude of houris, beautifully spotted; where jack rabbits that run fast but not too fast (like the houris) are as the sands of the desert; where each blissful hour is mealtime; where in long evenings there are a million fire-places with logs forever burning, and one curls oneself up and blinks into the flames and nods and dreams, remembering the old brave days on earth, and the love of one's Master and Mistress.

I am afraid this is too much for even such a dog as I am to expect. But peace, at least is certain. Peace and long rest for weary old heart and head and limbs, and eternal sleep in the earth I have loved so well. Perhaps, after all, this is best.

One last request I earnestly make. I have heard my Mistress say, "When Blemie dies we must never have another dog. I love him so much I could never love another one." Now I would ask her, for love of me, to have another. It would be a poor tribute to my memory never to have a dog again. What I would like to feel is that, having once had me in the family, now she cannot live without a dog! I have never had a narrow jealous spirit. I have always held that most dogs are good (and one cat, the black one I have permitted to share the living room rug during the evenings, whose affection I have tolerated in a kindly spirit, and in rare sentimental moods, even reciprocated a trifle). Some dogs, of course, are better than others. Dalmatians, naturally, as everyone knows, are best. So I suggest a Dalmatian as my successor. He can hardly be as well bred or as well mannered or as distinguished and handsome as I was in my prime. My Master and Mistress must not ask the impossible. But he will do his best, I am sure, and even his inevitable defects will help by comparison to keep my memory green. To him I bequeath my collar and leash and my overcoat and raincoat, made to order in 1929 at Hermès in Paris. He can never wear them with the distinction I did, walking around the Place Vendôme, or later along Park Avenue, all eyes fixed on me in admiration; but again I am sure he will do his utmost not to appear a mere gauche provincial dog. Here on the ranch, he may prove himself quite worthy of comparison, in some respects. He will, I presume, come closer to jack rabbits than I have been able to in recent years. And, for all his faults, I hereby wish him the happiness I know will be his in my old home.

One last word of farewell, Dear Master and Mistress. Whenever you visit my grave, say to yourselves with regret but also with happiness in your hearts at the remembrance of my long happy life with you: "Here lies one who loved us and whom we loved." No matter how deep my sleep I shall hear you, and not all the power of death can keep my spirit from wagging a grateful tail.

Bud Johns was still a teenager in the early 1940s when he was hired for his first job as a newspaper reporter. He sold his first magazine article later the same year and has been earning his living as a writer, editor and publisher ever since. *Old Dogs Remembered* is his fourth published book. It was preceded by *The Ombibulous Mr. Mencken, Bastard in the Ragged Suit* and *What Is This Madness?*

Old Dogs Remembered is dedicated to his wife, the writer Fran Moreland Johns. They live in San Francisco.